PERSEPHONE RETURNS

PERSEPHONE RETURNS

Victims, Heroes and the Journey from the Underworld

by

TANYA WILKINSON, PH.D.

PAGEMILL PRESS

A Division of Circulus Publishing Group, Inc.

Berkeley, California

PERSEPHONE RETURNS:
Victims, Heroes and the Journey from the Underworld

Publisher: Tamara Traeder
Editorial Director: Roy M. Carlisle
Copyeditor: Priscilla Stuckey
Cover Design: Big Fish Design
Interior Design: Gordon Chun Design
Typographic Specifications: Body text set in 11-point Adobe Caslon regular, chapter titles in 11-point Adobe Caslon bold, subheads in 9-point Frutiger Black

PRINTED IN THE UNITED STATES OF AMERICA
First Edition
9 8 7 6 5 4 3 2 1
99 98 97 96

LIBRARY OF CONGRESS CATALOGING-IN-PUBLICATION DATA
Wilkinson, Tanya, 1952–
Persephone returns : victims, heroes and the journey from the underworld / by Tanya Wilkinson. — 1st ed.
p. cm.
Includes bibliographical references (p. 230) and index.
ISBN: 1-879290-09-x (pbk.)
1. Adjustment (Psychology) 2. Psychic trauma. 3. Victims—Psychology. 4. Self-defeating behavior. 5. Jungian psychology. I. Title.
BF335.4.W55 1996
616.85′8—dc20 96-19832
CIP

Distributed to the trade by Publishers Group West

DEDICATION

Für Jürgen

VOR DEIN SPÄTES GESICHT

allein—
gängerisch zwischen
auch mich verwandelnden Nächten,
kam etwas zu stehen,
das schon einmal bei uns war, un—
berührt von Gedanken.

Paul Celan

AUTHOR'S NOTE

To preserve my psychotherapy clients' anonymity I have disguised and changed identifiable characteristics whenever possible. All of the clinical examples in this book are composite portraits, that is generalized descriptions that draw related points from several different clients' stories.

For instance, an issue that emerged in one person's psychotherapy might be included in a composite description in which some parts of the personal description given (such as profession, marital status, place of residence, ethnic background, gender) are different than the client's, as long as those aspects are not important to the central issues being discussed. In addition to protecting confidentiality more effectively, composites allow for more broadly applicable examples.

EDITOR'S NOTE

1. As writers, editors, and publishers we believe in the power of the written word and therefore assume our responsibility to use inclusive language is great. Our intention is clear: no person of either gender should feel excluded by or discriminated against because of language used in a PageMill Press book. If there is a gap between our intention and our practice we apologize. In the interests of careful scholarship the authors and editors have not always edited quotations by others whose language does not conform to our standards. We leave it to our discerning readers to decide if this practice enhances understanding or not.

2. In Chapter Eight of *Persephone Returns* the reader will notice the use of periodic bold superscript endnote numbers. These bold numbers denote discursive content in the note rather than the normal bibliographic endnote entry designated by regular superscript numbers.

CONTENTS

Preface

I never consciously intended to write a book about victim identities. Certainly I had given a lot of thought to the "victim issue" in connection with both my work and my world, but I had never focused on the idea of writing about victims. One day while I was sitting at my computer working on an essay about art that served only as compost for this book, I got up to answer the phone. It was a wrong number. When I returned to the computer, the outline of *Persephone Returns* was waiting to be typed. I felt that the idea for the book was visiting me for an afternoon and that I could take the hint or not. I took it.

The fact that I was even sitting at the computer that day had a great deal to do with the California Institute of Integral Studies, familiarly known as CIIS. I have been on the faculty of CIIS since 1980, and it has always been a place at which I could grow as a teacher. Around 1990 a new President, Robert McDermott, and a new Dean of Faculty, Jürgen Kremer, began to work on making the institute a place where faculty could also grow as writers. On the most fundamental level this involved changes in salary structure. Just as powerful for me, however, was a change in atmosphere and the formation of a faculty seminar, a germinal group for the writer in me, eventually known as the Dawn Seminar. This name was not a precious reference to the dawn of some new era but rather an acknowledgment of the ridiculously early hour of our meetings. Membership varied with the years, but Mike Acree, Daniel Deslauriers, Elinor Gadon, Don Johnson, Jürgen Kremer, Eva Leveton, and

Judy Schavrein formed the core of the seminar. They functioned variously as my encouragers, role models, critics, muses, and nemeses. It is safe to say that without them I would never have written anything. They were the first to see the outline of this book.

Roy M. Carlisle was the second. Roy had heard me lecture and had been encouraging me to write a book for some time. His response to the seed notion of *Persephone Returns* was immensely encouraging and bracingly practical. He is the editor of this volume, and he, together with Tamara Traeder, the publisher of PageMill Press, turned the writing and production of the book into a remarkable experience.

My psychotherapy clients, who are dedicated to the pursuit of self-understanding, made *Persephone Returns* possible in the most basic way. My practice of psychotherapy is at the root of my thought process, and it is the source of whatever insight I possess. My clients' willingness to explore, to trust the process of therapy, and to risk the Underworld make all of my work—therapy, teaching, consulting, and writing—possible and give it meaning. Some of my clients gave me permission to use parts of their stories in this book. In order to more thoroughly protect their privacy and in order to make the examples applicable to as broad a range of readers as possible, I have developed composite portraits. This means that each example represents more than one client who experienced similar, related dynamics. All of the personal data in the examples—name, profession, marital status, number of siblings, even age or gender—have been changed, except for those items that directly affect the issues being discussed.

Certain people were indispensable to me in their willingness to listen, read, reread, or proofread and in their determination to keep my book in their thoughts, regularly bringing the whole thing up even when it was the last thing I wanted to talk about. Marc Ellen Hamel, Robert Hopcke, Paul Schwartz, Padma Catell, John Dyckman, Pamela Colorado, Helen Wickes, Gail Grynbaum, Rusa Chiu, Inger Johanssen, and Jadwiga Rozanska helped to keep me on track in these and other, less tangible ways.

All of my faculty colleagues in the psychology program at CIIS supported my work and tolerated my distraction from other duties. Of these, Robert Morgan, the Program Director, deserves my particular thanks. I've never had a more supportive boss. The staff of CIIS also should be thanked for their devotion to the daily running of that unique institution. They support me in everything I do as a member of the faculty. My students at the institute, who are dedicated to questioning everything, have given me the opportunity (or perhaps forced me) to think through my assumptions and clarify my thoughts. They are a constant source of renewal and inspiration.

My mother, Helen Wilkinson, had an unwavering, clear faith in my ability and future. My father, Red Wilkinson, embodied and taught resilience in the way that he lived every day. My memory of their struggle not to be victimized by seemingly overwhelming circumstances informs this book. I wish they were here to read it (and, in my mother's case, to give me a piece of her mind about certain parts).

Finally, I am thankful for and to my oldest friends who are collectively, if somewhat bizarrely, known as The Clump. Over the past twenty years (and in some cases more) they have put up with a great deal from me in one way and another. Yet from Thanksgiving to Thanksgiving they remain faithful and true. In a cold world it helps to know of one place that is always warm and where, at some point in the evening, there will be dancing.

CHAPTER ONE

THE BATTLE OF OPPOSITES

Story as a Middle Way

When I asked my brother what he thought
about the way Father used to beat me up he said,
"I thought you didn't run fast enough."

Jane, a client in psychotherapy, was beginning to talk to her family about the constant violence of her childhood. As I listened, my anger grew. How far would the family go in its efforts to trivialize the reality of this woman's victimization? What bogus and blaming rationalizations had she heard again and again? What insinuations had Jane internalized so that she now repeated within herself the basic disfiguring lie—that she had somehow been responsible for her father's berserk rages? At the same time I knew that she had not tried to run faster, while her siblings had. As an adult she still does not run fast enough when confronted with abuse. Like Persephone, Jane had been caught, dragged down against her will, and like Persephone, she eventually ate the food of the Underworld and began to spend a part of her life there.[1]

The truth ignored in her brother's words: no child should have to run for her life. The truth addressed in her brother's words: she accepted her victimization then and participates in it now. How can these truths be reconciled?

The Cycle of Blame

Twenty years ago the feminist movement began to challenge society's tendency to ignore the truth of victimization. Blaming the victim has been slowly losing its automatic legitimacy as a rationalization for exploitation and as an excuse for denying protection to the vulnerable and threatened. As Judith Herman, a psychiatrist who specializes in researching and treating the effects of abuse, points out in *Trauma and Recovery,* recognition of victimization and its effects has been cyclical in Western culture, and such recognition is always connected to a political movement that strives to raise consciousness.[2] The existencc of trauma and of its damaging effects remains the same, but our culture's willingness to acknowledge those effects develops only when pushed by a political movement whose agenda includes rectifying some particular victimizing condition. Why is it necessary to actively raise consciousness about something as obvious as the fact that no child should have to run in mortal fear from a parent? What makes it necessary to push for awareness of the blatant psychological injury caused by such experiences?

The tendency to suppress awareness of victimization and to ignore the consequences of trauma coexists with a predisposition toward ignoring the inevitability of human vulnerability. On an individual and cultural level Western people, and perhaps especially American people, cling to the image of a hero, a person who, as a consequence of being good or strong, cannot really be hurt. That image could be called a hero persona, using C. G. Jung's concept of the persona as a mask or mantle that covers the self.[3] The persona is useful in performing social roles, but if an individual conflates a persona with his or her identity, the normal evolution of the personality may be deformed. The specifics of the hero persona vary according to family and gender role expectations, but the fantasy of invulnerability through some form of perfection is consistent. If I strive to be good or heroic or strong, I will not be hurt. When I am hurt it is because I have failed in my pursuit of the ideal.

Thus when Sula, another client, is verbally attacked by her unpredictably irrational and irritable boss, she fantasizes that, if her performance becomes perfect in every detail, her supervisor will become calm and beneficent. It does not occur to Sula that her boss's moods are her boss's responsibility or that the imposition of those moods on employees is unfair. Sula works extra hours, loses sleep in worry, expends heroic effort to perfect her skills—all to no avail. The shield of the hero persona, in the image of the faultless worker, fails to protect Sula from her supervisor's random attacks. Sula redoubles her efforts. Within this view of self and world the appropriate response to abuse, exploitation, and oppression is to uphold the heroic ideal and try to achieve safety by struggling for the ideal—to blame the self for the failure of the hero persona in controlling abuse. If one cannot triumph in that struggle, one may deserve to be hurt.

The hero persona as a complex of beliefs, feelings, and reactions has many consequences. The fantasy of the ideal person who is too good to be hurt, or at least too good to stay hurt, protects abusive and tyrannical people from the consequences of their actions by placing total responsibility for injury on the injured. Personal identification with the image of the hero as the ideal self predisposes victims to accept blame. It predisposes people to blame others who are victimized. On a cultural level, identification with the hero persona encourages a picture of life that excludes normal human vulnerability. The large-scale fantasy is that anyone who strives to embody the hero can triumph over adversity, oppression, and abuse. Conversely, those who have manifestly failed to triumph—battered women, victims of gay bashing, teenage mothers, drug addicts, and so forth—have brought on their own fate through failure to strive. If Rocky can be reduced to degradation in movie after movie, only to triumph again by the final frame through his persistence and grit, isn't that indomitable path open to everyone? The concept of circumstances beyond individual control is unaddressed in this fantasy. Cultural identification with the hero persona powerfully skews both our perception and our judgment in relationship to abuse and victimization.

Revisioning and Backlash

It takes a powerful and consistent attack to dislodge the heroic ideal and foster awareness of abuse and its consequences. Feminism has led such an attack in the last twenty years. Beginning with an analysis of the impact of rape on the victim, feminist activists, therapists, and writers began to insist on acknowledging abuse and oppression, to challenge victim-blaming, and to pursue the social and political rectification of the conditions and consequences of abuse.[4] Over time a theoretical framework was developed that revisioned the definition of abuse and the cultural meaning of victimization. This framework gave rise to a new understanding and analysis, eventually providing a conceptual foundation for victims of abuse and oppression in their struggle to become aware of the effects of their experiences. That awareness fostered individual and group efforts to direct anger toward the abuser and/or oppressor and to pursue the rectification of injuries on both personal and political levels. These efforts became an integral part of feminist, minority, and gay activism and provided a basis for child abuse intervention and the treatment of adult survivors of childhood abuse. Activism has further raised consciousness, encouraging the continuous refinement and elaboration of a worldview that challenges our culture's identification with the hero ideal. Books, articles, entire publications, innumerable support groups, lobbying efforts, and changes in the law and standards of social behavior have flowed from this revisioning of the dynamics of victimization.

This revisioning has engendered a backlash, which comes from many angles. Camille Paglia, Kate Roiphe, and others scorn the "victim culture" of feminism.[5] Social critic Stanley Crouch sarcastically rails, "Blessed are the victims, the new catechism taught, for their suffering has illuminated them and they shall lead us to the light, even as they provide magnets for our guilt."[6] Wendy Kaminer (author of *I'm Dysfunctional, You're Dysfunctional*) attacks self-help organizations as inherently debilitating.[7] The title of Charles Sykes's book, *A Nation of Victims: The Decay of the American Character,* sums up the essence of backlash commentary—particularly the tendency to frame that commentary in moralistic terms of decadence.[8] In this analysis the victim is seen as manipulative and childish (whiny, demanding) whenever he or she is engaged in identifying abuse and its effects. An accompanying perception or perhaps suspicion is that instances of abuse are fabricated or exaggerated in order to avoid personal responsibility, maintain a franchise on unreasonable entitlement, or pursue covert power.

A Nation of Victims has gained considerable currency in the national debate and for excellent reason. Sykes vividly describes the debilitating effects of attachment to a victim identity, though he does not use that term.[9] His rallying cry concerning character holds a necessary seed of truth, in the sense that victims do hold the source of transformation within themselves. However, his notion of the type of character required for freedom from victim identification is not particularly useful or accurate.

Backlash commentators like Sykes strive to resurrect the hero persona. Why don't victims of sexual harassment simply yell at their harassers? Paglia wants to know; that's what she did. The supposition here is that everyone has equal access to power and equal ability to use it. If you lack either access to power or the ability to use power, it's your personal failure. Strive to correct that failure, and you will never be victimized. Learn to run faster, as Jane's brother might say. In most instances victim commentary is transparently political in its motivation. As A. S. Ross, a journalist who has analyzed the victim discourse, points out, conservatives like Sykes only discuss the victim culture of marginal groups.[10] These backlash commentators do not notice, for example, the whining of big businessmen who claim that their failures spring from being victimized by the Japanese or by the unions.

Although deformed by a variety of biases and covert purposes, the backlash commentary touches on a spark of truth. As C. G. Jung pointed out, extremes tend to flip over into their opposites. The extremes of hero personae have flipped over into extremes of victim personae, producing situations in which individuals or groups become victim-identified. When Sykes says, "Victimism debilitates its practitioners by trapping them in a world of oppressive demons," he touches on a reality of victim identification familiar to many psychotherapists.[11] The polarized, self-righteous and political nature of the current discourse on victimization makes an open-ended examination of such victim identification difficult. Tragically, neither the hero nor the victim persona addresses some important realities of abuse and victimization. Neither helps us to understand the contradictions inherent in, for instance, Jane's past and present.

The Victim Persona

People who have been victimized, whether individually or in the social-political arena, do sometimes become immersed and trapped in a victim persona. This is very rarely a manipulative choice, as the "victim culture" commentators imagine it. Nor is maintaining a victim identity useful in fighting abuse and oppression. The individual so identified tends to become more and more internally weakened by the persona, obsessed by its drama. Others tend to perceive and experience a victim-identified person as dismissable, thus impairing that person's impact on external circumstances. In the polarized debate over victims, neither side tries to delineate the spiritual and psychological paths that allow an individual to confront the reality of abuse and its effects without becoming victim-identified.

Difficult as it may be to accept, some experiences of abuse are not directly rectifiable. There are situations in which no amount of personal or group empowerment, no striving for the hero persona, can shift the external circumstances of abuse or oppression. The "normal" cultural method of resolving an abusive situation, that is, the pursuit of justice and/or revenge, may not be available or may offer only partial results. In those instances, what internal paths are available to the victims of abuse so that their fundamental identity and experience of life is not controlled or destroyed by the oppressive circumstances? How can someone who has been victimized deal directly with the pragmatic, psychological, and emotional effects of the victimization without assuming a victim identity?

Such questions fit neither the hero nor the victim persona. The public debate makes little room in its rhetoric for the psychological complexity of victimization. Most analyses ignore the fact that many people are both victim and abuser. The all-good, all-innocent victim is a fantasy indulged in by all parties. From the perspective of those identified with the hero persona, only the pure and innocent can be actual victims, worthy of rescue. Any evidence of inconsistent, self-serving, or negative behavior impugns the reality of the claimed abuse. For example, Anita Hill's inconsistent behavior in staying professionally connected to Clarence Thomas allowed the Senate Judiciary Committee to bypass the issue of investigating Thomas's behavior and concentrate instead on Hill's character.

From the point of view of those identified with the victim persona, abuse or even the possibility of abuse imbues the victim or victim group with de facto innocence, and any effort to examine shadowy behavior on the victim's part is tantamount to blaming the victim. This dynamic can be seen in examples ranging from the Tawana Brawley scandal[12] to the furor engendered by criticism of Israel. Coming from either end of the spectrum, the image of the pure victim leaves the real victim entirely alone with his or her complicated, multidimensional, far-from-pure experience.

Expressions of opinion in the dialogue on victimization and abuse share certain characteristics, regardless of the political or moral stance being expressed. Black-and-white thinking predominates in the debate. Those who support and pursue the concerns and rights of victims as well as those who see that concern as destructive to "character" use the rhetoric of blame, sin, and retribution. Pundits from both poles of the discourse tend to insist that the issue can be fully resolved through the control of external behavior, though always the behavior of someone other than the speaker. Attention to the internal experience of abuse is frequently construed as an attempt to ignore the importance of outward action. Gloria Steinem's struggle with internalized oppression, detailed in her book *Revolution from Within,*[13] was equated by some feminists with "betraying" the call for social action, as though the internal and external processes were mutually exclusive. At the same time, critics from the opposite end of the spectrum condemned the book as a prime example of glorifying the victim role. Introspection is denigrated from both directions; concrete action is spoken of as though it were distinct from consciousness.[14]

Behavior is, of course, quite important. Action is critical. People need to be able to speak up for themselves, name injustice, fight for justice, request help and legal protection, organize and act in groups to affect society, challenge authority, listen to challenges from others, and so forth. But what does it mean that in the victim dialogue most of the action called for must be taken by someone other than the speaker and his or her group? Solutions are typically and exclusively spoken of as acts that must be undertaken by someone else. Some say victims must rectify their own injuries, a stance exemplified by Shelby Steele's analysis of the experience of racial insults as an internal "recomposition" performed by the one who feels insulted, who must then eliminate the feeling of being insulted through their own process.[15] Conversely, others demand that authority figures remove the circumstances of abuse, perhaps by making racial insults into "hate crimes." Neither camp reflects on its own behavior. Action to be taken by the speaker and his or her affiliated group is usually action designed to force the "other" to behave correctly. When the "other" does not act in the demanded way, he or she is vilified in self-righteous, frequently melodramatic terms, a process commonly referred to as demonization. Demonization is inevitably accompanied by beatification. If one participant in a conflict is saddled with all the evil traits, his or her opponent tends to acquire a one-sided angelic glow.

Language and Projection

The language of demonization is the language of projection. The disquieting, ugly aspects of victimization are perceived as manifesting solely in the "other," who must change them. For those identified with the hero persona the shadowy aspects of abuse are weakness, indirectness, vulnerability to injury, and need for protection. These are projected onto perceived victims as moral defects. Within this worldview, Hedda Nussbaum (the common-law wife of Joel Steinberg, who passively stood by while he beat their adopted daughter to death), a woman disfigured by facial beatings and drugged into submission to her murderous husband, can be seen as simply a bad mother.[16] Or a naked, bleeding teenager can be sent back into Jeffrey Dahmer's apartment by the police, his obvious disorientation and distress becoming a subject for homophobic jokes on the police radio.[17] For those identified with the victim persona, the traits that are denied include the desires for power, dominance, and revenge. These are projected onto perceived abusers as sins.

The hallmark of projection is its one-sidedness. The projectee may or may not have some of the projected traits. Projection is present not in the issue of accuracy but in the fact that the projector rejects all personal connection to the projected traits. The portrait is of demons, saints, and martyrs rather than of complex human beings who, as human beings, must share many internal characteristics.

The defensive nature of projection is apparent; the projector need never confront his or her own shadow. Instead she feels virtuous in contrast to the projectee and relieved of the horror of the projectee's experience (as in "I'm a much better person than Nussbaum, I don't need to think about her life"). The shadow, as used here, denotes unacknowledged and disdained aspects of the personality, which are split off into the unconscious. When the ego, the conscious aspect of the Self, identifies with a hero persona, awareness of the experience of victimization is pushed out of consciousness and must reside in the shadow.

Adherents of the hero persona see themselves as heroic and see victims as morally deficient, but those adherents, in turn, are seen by victims as abusive. Adherents of the victim persona see themselves as outraged innocents but are perceived from the opposite side as, once again, abusive. Both sides maintain their identification with the chosen persona by projecting the shadow onto the opposing side. Interactions based on projection fail. Polarization is inevitable, and debate tends to degenerate into a competition for the moral high ground, characterized by strenuous efforts to force the other to admit demon status.

What does the nature of the rhetoric surrounding victims mean? What underlying factors are implied by the characteristics of that rhetoric? The avoidance of introspection, emphasis on constant action, and tendency toward black-and-white thinking militate against self-awareness. The eradication of complexity and the illusion of sure simplicity leave the ego with a brittle, inflexible stance toward experience. The constant use of quasi-moral and religious language, the processes of demonization and beatification, seem to indicate the presence of a spiritual issue, and one that carries a potent charge. The recurrent ideal images of pure victim and invulnerable hero hint at the activation of archetypal energies.

The archetypes are deep, underlying structures that provide the psyche with a language of images. All of human experience, according to Jung, springs from an archetypal core, but it is in spiritual or religious experience that we can most clearly see the psychological action of the archetype. "Archetypes are the primary forms that govern the psyche, but they cannot be contained only by the psyche since they manifest as well in physical, social, linguistic, aesthetic and spiritual modes."[18] Access to the archetypal level of experience presents a two-edged possibility: a balanced, sturdy, and flexible ego will benefit from the transformative power of the archetype, while a brittle or unbalanced ego will be inflated by its intense energy. Normally the archetypal core of intense primordial energy and imagery is mediated by personal awareness, interpersonal relationships, social constructs, and cultural meanings. These are essentially containers which help to bring the ego and the archetype into a dialectical relationship. When archetypal aspects of experience are activated, intense emotion is inevitable. If the individual does not have the ego skills and interpersonal relationships necessary to hold and process such strong feelings, they will be projected onto others. If a culture does not have the social structures and beliefs necessary to hold and understand these intense emotions on a collective level, then they will flow into destructive conflict.

When the "containers" of personal awareness and cultural meanings break down, as they have in the victim discourse, unmediated archetypal energies inflate human experience, promoting distorted perception and extreme behavior at the personal and collective levels. The Salem witch hunts and the Nazi era are both examples of social and political situations in which archetypal images of evil and purity were invoked and, consequently, unmediated archetypal energies infused culture, fueling a battle of seeming opposites.

The powerful, archetypal opposites at work in our culture's victim debate and in the individual who is struggling with an experience of victimization are difficult to contain. Intellectual insight alone is inadequate to the task of investigating the profound meaning and impact of these experiences. We need an approach that will give us access to the personal and transpersonal resources of the Self, resources that can contain the opposites, allowing an exploration that is not distorted by polarization.

The Power of Story

What method of investigation will allow us effectively to explore these underlying factors and their interaction? Is it possible to explore the victim experience without falling into one of the opposed camps? The heavily politicized and polarized public debate makes new insight difficult. Reactivity, preconception, and dependence on received wisdom run high. The topic of victimization also activates unconscious processes and defenses, making open-minded investigation difficult, as we have seen. In addition, our culture is predisposed to favor analyses that are pragmatic and concrete, a predisposition that tends to skew exploration toward premature problem-solving and away from the potentially messy contradictions of inner life. We may be able to avoid these pitfalls through the use of story.

Stories, and most particularly myths and fairy tales, can provide an entrance into the Underworld life of phenomena. The intensity of the victim debate, with its distortions, volatile emotions, and melodramatic style, taps the depths of inner life and experience. Narrative and image are gateways to those depths, connecting habitual workaday consciousness to realms of human experience that are neither cognitive in nature nor accessible to cognitive modes. The portraits of victims and the explications of victims' lives in archetypal stories lead us into open exploration, activating our search for meaning and self-knowledge. Such stories easily hold the contradictions and oppositions inherent in profound human experiences, helping us avoid the temptation to polarize into simplistic, projection-laden analyses. "Story is the linguistic form closest to bone and to cosmic vision."[19]

The myth is a form of imaginal "knowing" that is more expansive and multilayered than linear, rational knowing. A myth that resonates with the emotional and psychological situation gives us a felt experience of archetypal power. Myths and fairy tales weave together the material, psychological, and spiritual worlds, allowing us to keep the reality of the interconnections alive in our understanding. Because mythic narratives function metaphorically rather than rationally, they are particularly effective in providing access to the wholeness that is potential in the archetypal Self. According to Jung, we may define the Self

> as the totality of the conscious and unconscious psyche, but this totality transcends our vision. . . . It would be wildly arbitrary to restrict the Self to the limits of the individual psyche, quite apart from the fact that we have not the least knowledge of those limits, seeing that they also lie in the unconscious. . . . we should not be surprised if the empirical manifestations of unconscious contents bear all the marks of something illimitable, something not determined by time and space.[20]

As is clear from this statement, the Self is both personal and transpersonal, a resource of transformative power and unique individuality, and we gain access to it through the unconscious.

The transcendent power and the visionary quality of encounters with the Self tend to lead people to use exalted language when describing such encounters. The main problem for the theorist, writer, and therapist is to find a medium, a way of expressing the felt truths encountered in the unconscious; the medium must be faithful to the experience but accessible to everyday consciousness. The ego and the body live in the everyday world, and they must be able to hold onto nourishment from the Self in that everyday world. Archetypal stories provide both access to the deep unconscious and a medium for containing and processing what is brought up from the depths. Myths, fairy tales, and dreams depict, in narrative and image, the nature and effects of encounters with the Self. The personal and transpersonal resources of the Self which lie hidden in the depths of the unconscious can enable the ego to transcend polarization and to grapple with shadow material without resorting to projection.

Access to the unconscious requires an encounter with the shadow, the rejected part of the personality that lies at the entrance to the unconscious. Profound psychological and emotional experiences such as those produced by the trauma of victimization involve confronting both the personal and collective shadows; such experiences can be, in essence, a descent into the unconscious. The trauma of the descent may cause the ego to try to recover through identifying with either a victim or hero persona. This is a regressive and brittle solution to the challenge presented by the descent. Alternatively, the descent may lead to an experience of the Self, which can provide the container and resources to address the powerful dynamics at work in the victim experience. According to Marie-Louise von Franz, myths and fairy tales tell us, in symbolic language and from a variety of angles, the story of the Self.[21] Delving into the archetypal stories in the following chapters will give us some guidance in our effort to bring the descent of the victim into a transformative context, a context that includes the Self.

Methodological Considerations

Each chapter in this book describes a form of victim identification, as experienced from within and as perceived from without. I begin with stories from myth or fairy tale that embody the archetypal aspect of each identity, I then give clinical anecdotes, discuss the psychodynamics of becoming trapped in each persona, and indicate examples from popular culture. Individuals may experience any or all of the dynamics of different stories at different times and in different moods. Sometimes a person's inner world will correspond vividly to one tale. "This is *my* story," the gut says. Other times a piece of one story and a fragment of another speak to the individual. The unconscious is boundaryless; its parts overlap one another. To form a conscious relationship to unconscious material, one must follow distinct threads, explicating and becoming conscious of them as fully as possible. At the same time one must maintain an awareness of the overall web and its interconnections. In practice this means that while we explore each story for its unique insight, we acknowledge and benefit from the ways in which images overlap and amplify one another. The following categorized explorations of archetypal stories are meant to inspire connection to the imaginal world and facilitate self-awareness, not confine that inner world through overly rigid descriptions and prescriptive definitions. To state this more simply, it is appropriate to use any part of any story that fits and feels helpful. Learning from the imagination does not require or benefit from a rigid approach.

I want to emphasize that the chapters on victim identities do not constitute an inclusive typology of victim psychology. They are not an alternative diagnostic system in the making. The story chapters are explorations, and they are meant to inspire and guide the reader's unique, personal explorations. Emerson said, "Do not require a description of the countries toward which you sail. The description does not describe them to you and tomorrow you arrive there and know them by inhabiting them." Each individual Self is a country that must be inhabited to be known. My hope is that the work I do with myths and fairy tales can be used as an aid to sailing rather than as a prescription for concrete actions. I understand the desire for prescribed remedies. A concrete, directed course of action would be greatly comforting in dealing with the highly charged and complex victim experience. However, the desire to squash that complex experience into neat and tidy explanations is, in part, responsible for our society's failure to develop a workable response to the victim's experience.

In approaching the stories I move from insights provided by the narrative imagery of the fairy tale to clinical material and back again. This method grounds the symbolic, archetypal material in personal experience and connects the personal to its numinous source. (The Latin term *numen* means divine, in this case referring to the transpersonal aspects of the Self.) A complex interweaving of internal states and external circumstances produces a victim identification. Moving between story and clinical material allows us to explore internal and external aspects of the victim identity in a way that reflects this interweaving. The classic Jungian view is that archetypal tales reveal the unfolding of the inner journey: the dramatis personae are analyzed as aspects of the Self. For the most part I agree with this view and believe that the transformations depicted in each story are ultimately psychological transformations of inner reality, reflecting profound changes in the relationships between persona and shadow, ego and unconscious. However, the social, cultural, and familial power structures, the external forces that generate and support victim identities, must be addressed in our analyses as well. The episodes of the stories provide an opportunity to discuss the development of the child's identification with a victim persona, the way that identity persists and affects adult life, the resulting internal configuration of the psyche, the sources of attachment to this victim identity, and finally, the form of the victim persona's possible transformation.

The psychological terminology used here is derived from C. G. Jung's personality theory.[22] The ego is the central organizing complex of the conscious aspect of the psyche. The shadow is "an unconscious part of the personality characterized by traits and attitudes which the . . . ego tends to reject."[23] When the word Self is capitalized it refers to Jung's particular definition, on which we have already touched.

When *self* is not capitalized it is being used colloquially. Throughout, I use the terms *victim identity* and *victim persona* interchangeably.

As with all archetypal stories, the tales used in this book have great depth and lend themselves to many useful interpretations. The fact that I use a story to reflect on the dynamics of a particular victim persona does not mean that this is the only way to view that story. Working with myths and fairy tales helps us to draw on resources within the unconscious. Those resources are universal in the sense that anyone and everyone can gain internal access to them. At the same time the paths to those resources of the unconscious are very particular to the individual. This is the paradoxical nature of the Self. The stories I have chosen to work with give us images for the universal dimensions of these resources. The reader's own personal story must be told and explored, reflected on with the same respect as the archetypal tale. Only this will reveal the individual path that will be most helpful to each person.

CHAPTER TWO

VICTIM AS BETRAYED INNOCENT

The Rape of Persephone

KORE, the maiden, was picking fragrant flowers in a meadow. She reached for the narcissus, and the earth suddenly opened wide. Out of the depths came a golden chariot drawn by black horses and driven by the faceless Lord of the Underworld. "Mother, Mother," she screamed, "help me!" But Demeter, her mother, was far away. No one heard her cries, except for old Hecate in her cave, who hurried to the rescue but could find no sign of Kore.

Demeter sought Kore for nine days and nights. She dressed in mourning and called out for her daughter ceaselessly, refusing to eat, drink, or rest. On the tenth day Demeter came in disguise to the city of Eleusis, appearing to be an old woman. The king and his wife welcomed her into their household, and she offered to nurse their infant son, Demophoön. The children and servants of the house exerted themselves to bring the old nurse (as they saw her) out of her sadness, eventually coaxing her to laugh and to drink barley-water. Demeter tried to reciprocate by making Demophoön immortal but was interrupted in her spell and the baby died. Thwarted in her effort to keep him from death, she was enraged.

Soon after Demophoön's death the swineherd of the King's household told Demeter of a great split in the earth that swallowed his swine. A chariot appeared from the direction of Eleusis and dashed down the chasm. The chariot driver's face was invisible and he had a shrieking girl clasped in his right arm. Armed with this evidence, Demeter and Hecate confronted Helios, the sun, who sees all, and forced him to admit that Hades was the villain, doubtless with the connivance of his brother Zeus, King of the Gods. Even though Zeus was Demeter's brother and Kore's father he was ignoring Demeter's grief and Hades's crime.

Demeter continued to wander the earth, forbidding the trees to yield fruit and the herbs to grow, until the human race stood in danger of extinction and there were no sacrifices for the Gods. Only one course of action remained for Zeus. He sent Hermes with a message to Hades, telling him to restore Kore to her mother. He sent a message to Demeter, saying, "You will have your daughter again, provided she has not tasted the food of the dead."

However, Hades's gardeners had seen Kore eat seven seeds of a pomegranate. Based on this, Hades claimed Kore as his own, and Demeter prepared to continue blighting the Earth. Zeus asked Rhea, the mother of Hades, Demeter, and himself, to mediate, and at last a compromise was reached. Kore would spend three months of the year with Hades, reigning as Persephone, Queen of the Underworld. During that time the earth would be barren, mourning the loss of Persephone. The remaining nine months of the year Persephone dwells with Demeter and the earth is fertile. Hecate agreed to oversee the arrangement, making sure that it was kept, and watching over Persephone while she resides in the Underworld.

The innocent idyll of Persephone's childhood is shattered by her incestuous uncle, Hades the Lord of the Underworld. Her mother, Demeter, cannot save her. Her father, Zeus, King of the Gods, conspires in her betrayal. No one hears her cries. The myth begins as a classic tale of the victimization of an innocent child, a victimization and betrayal that determines the child's fate. The story is also a template for transformation in the Underworld. Contemplating the myth of Persephone, "We realize the universal principle of life, which is to be pursued, to be robbed, raped, to fail to understand, to rage and to grieve but then . . . to be born again."[1] To descend and to return.

A descent to the Underworld is one of the oldest and most common of mythic motifs. Descents follow an overall structure, beginning with a separation from known life, followed by a descent to the land of the dead, and ending with a return to the Upperworld in a changed state. It is a structure that follows the typical form of an initiation, a rite of passage. This kind of journey has been written of in Joseph Campbell's *Hero with a Thousand Faces* as an archetypal hero's journey [2] and in Sylvia Perera's *Descent to the Goddess* as an archetypal woman's journey.[3] Persephone's descent is a victim's journey. She does not choose her descent, as heroes do or as the old Great Goddesses (like Inanna in Perera's study) did. Her initiation into the Underworld is the victim's initiation: an abduction, a betrayal of innocence that all victims experience. At the same time Demeter is initiated, through her daughter's abduction, into the Underworld of loss and grief.

Upperworld and Underworld are strictly separated at the beginning of this myth. Kore is abruptly taken from a sunny, idyllic life above ground into an unknown hell. Seeing Upperworld and Underworld as mutually exclusive realities is one important factor in both the personal and cultural construction of the victim identity. In the Upperworld of our society the hero persona reigns, delineating our worldview. The ego ideal of the typical individual conforms to that Upperworld view. Normal human vulnerability is repressed for the sake of maintaining at least an appearance of the hero persona. In the Underworld of American culture and in the unconscious of the individual, the repressed vulnerability lives in the form of victim personae. These seeming opposites, the hero in the light of day and the victim relegated to the shadows, appear to be mutually exclusive, unreconcilable both in cultural discourse, as we have seen, and in the individual psyche, in the internal Upperworld of ego consciousness and Underworld of the unconscious. In some situations and in some people the poles of these opposites are reversed and the victim persona dominates consciousness. However, the split remains intact, even if turned upside down. After Kore is transformed into Persephone by the resolution of the conflict between

Demeter and Hades, she becomes a bridge between Upperworld and Underworld. Her descent and return allow her to traverse the split, connecting the two worlds.

Persephone is initiated, through her descent and return, into a new identity that can contain and negotiate the opposites of Upperworld and Underworld. We think of initiations as intentional rites of passage for which the initiate goes through extensive preparation. The preparation of the initiate provides him or her with guidance for a successful completion of the descent-and-return cycle of initiation. However, life itself administers initiations to both the prepared and the unprepared.[4] The majority of people in our culture who receive an initiation into the descent of victimization are children who are, of course, unprepared. Their descent into hell persists in adulthood as an entrapment of a part of the Self in an unconscious Underworld. Their culture provides them with little or no guidance for completing their initiation—for returning from the descent to a new identity. The predominant heroic ideal provides only stoicism or vengeance as ways to resolve victimization. These responses do not foster a real return. Rather, they freeze the victim experience in place as the central fact of identity. The way in which Demeter and Kore move through their initiation and descent and transform the betrayal of their innocence can provide a different guidance, forming a kind of retroactive preparation for the initiatory descent of victimization. Persephone returns, not as the nameless Kore-Maiden, the unconscious, suffering child, but as Queen of the Underworld.

A Myth for Women and Men

Demeter, Hecate, and Kore, who comes to be called Persephone, are a form of the three-in-one Goddess, an ancient pre-Christian trinity. Some mythologists, beginning with Robert Graves in *The White Goddess,*[5] have focused on the mother (Demeter), crone (Hecate), and maiden (Kore) aspects of the Triple Goddess as crucial only to the psychology of women. For Jung, "Demeter and Kore . . . extend feminine consciousness . . . widen out the narrowly limited conscious mind bound in space and time, give it intimations of a greater and more comprehensive personality which has a share in the eternal course of things."[6] Is this true only for "feminine consciousness"? Is it important only for women?

Certainly some aspects of this rich story speak to women in a special way. The Homeric "Hymn to Demeter," the earliest known version of the story of the Rape of Persephone, "seems to stress that the mysteries emerge from the private and even secret world of female experience."[7] However, it is no accident that both men and women were initiated into the Eleusinian Mysteries, the rituals used by the ancient Greeks to participate in the story of Persephone's descent and return. Kore is the part of the Self that is innocence betrayed, the Divine Child dragged down into the Underworld and ultimately transformed there. This is a fundamental human experience, transcending gender, class, and ethnicity. However, the patriarchal biases of Greek culture, biases that still shape most of our cultural perceptions concerning gender, have a great deal to do with the gender configurations in this myth.

The hero/victim split is associated with culture's masculine/feminine split. Therefore symbolic embodiments of the victim's journey of descent and return have a particular gender configuration. The heroic stance, which dominates our Upperworld, is strongly associated with values perceived as masculine. The victim position, with its vulnerability and helplessness, is identified with the feminine (in classical Greece and now) so that those who are victimized in our culture, whether they are male or female, are struggling with an experience that has a feminine cast. Although the archetypal journey of descent and return is common to all, at least potentially, a descent into the Underworld of victimization is an encounter with experiences and aspects of the Self that are strongly linked to the construct of femininity. Women hold a cultural position as the "carriers" of patriarchal society's unsolved problems,[8] and this position carries over into the symbolic realm. The unsolved problem here is that the values of the heroic ideal fail to address effectively the experiences of the victim. Feminine archetypal figures carry this problem in their stories, which attempt to solve or mitigate the imbalance psychologically, through symbol and metaphor.

The rape of Persephone shows us, in no uncertain terms, that there are tears in the fabric of life that can never be completely repaired, directions taken that, even if unchosen and unfair, can never be fully reversed because the self is changed by them. Even the most forceful, dedicated, and loving efforts, such as those undertaken by Demeter on behalf of Kore, cannot completely undo a descent to the Underworld. By tracing Demeter's transformation through grief and anger, by exploring Kore's transformation into Persephone, and by treating the characters in the myth as aspects of a Self that is both personal and transpersonal, we can uncover psychological insights that are useful to both men and women.

Innocence Betrayed

Persephone is called Kore, "the maiden," in the beginning of the story, and this alerts us to her intense vulnerability. In Western cultures the maiden embodies innocence, and Kore, picking flowers in a meadow, is emblematic of the kind of innocence that deserves protection. At this stage she seems to have few personal qualities, not even a real name. She is "the maiden," and as such she constellates that quality of fresh potential and unsullied grace that we so often see in young children and which Western culture tends to associate especially with virginal girls. As an image of the Divine Child, she "is a symbol of future hopes, the seedling, the potentiality of life, newness."[9] In C.G. Jung's essay on the archetype of the Divine Child he touches on the way in which "abandonment, exposure, danger" are inevitable conditions for the development of the archetype's potential.[10] Kore's abandonment, exposure, and danger spring from the betrayal of her innocence by her father and uncle, Zeus and Hades. This is the beginning of her descent and the condition of her transformation. As Kore she is the Divine Child, a spark of specialness which is suppressed in the Underworld waiting to be developed. This is one of the archetypal underpinnings fueling the intensity of the victim debate.

Kore's association with frivolity and pleasure is a key aspect of her innocence. She neither spins nor toils but gathers flowers. She plucks a narcissus just before her abduction, and this choice of flower may be metaphorically instructive. Kore is immersed in an enclosed world of enjoyment. She is self-absorbed and normally narcissistic, in the way of a prized child. Some psychological commentaries have tried to interpret the appearance of the narcissus at this crucial point as an indication of cause and effect, as though Kore's self-absorption brings Hades up from the Underworld. This view implies that Hades can be avoided by careful behavior, i.e., that he would not have abducted Kore if she were not self-absorbed. This notion runs counter to the essential point of the story's beginning, which is the inevitable, unavoidable loss of innocence, the end of innocent, healthy narcissism such as children experience, the end of the self-absorbed, protected world of childhood.

Sula, a psychotherapy client I have already mentioned, was a prized and praised child. Her parents, particularly her father, viewed her as a wonder child who could give the family a measure of glory. She would provide, through her wonderful attributes, a sense of meaning and purpose that her parents lacked, both individually and as a couple. She was to be a Divine Child for them. Nonetheless, Sula was left unprotected at crucial times in her infancy and childhood, including a period of time in the care of an abusive nanny. Even more importantly her pain was left uncomforted, for as a wonder child, she was supposed to be able to handle whatever happened without parental help. As a consequence, in adulthood Sula developed an obsession with protection, vulnerability, and safety; this obsession lay at the heart of her drive to be perfect. She obsessively pursued protection through perfectionism. She searched constantly for the personal flaws that, in her view, had caused her to be endangered in childhood and in the present. The relentless drive to be perfect, and thus perfectly protected, eventually rendered her life as barren and lifeless as Demeter's withdrawal rendered the Earth. Joy, spontaneity, and especially sexuality were experienced by Sula as disruptive harbingers of chaos.

Sula could not come to terms with the unpredictable nature of life or with the normalcy of human vulnerability. The myth of Persephone presents us with the fact that a person can, through no action of his or her own, be targeted for the most devastating attacks; neither manifest innocence, nor striving for perfection, nor access to powerful others is sufficient to completely protect anyone. As the daughter of extremely powerful parents, Kore should be well protected, but she is not. Everyone is vulnerable, and in this story, Hades symbolizes the overwhelming disintegrative Underworld forces to which we all are vulnerable.

In Greek myth as a whole Hades has a punctilious possessiveness concerning his dominion and prerogatives, combined with a tendency to complain. Overall the modern reader is tempted to see Hades as a faceless but remorseless rule-loving bureaucrat. One could easily envision him as an IRS auditor, giving new perspective to the inevitability of death and taxes. Hades employs a variety of petty, read-the-fine-print rules to exert his will, most of which work only in a partial manner. The issue of Persephone eating the seeds of the pomegranate is an example of the importance to Hades of seemingly minor infractions.

This aspect of Hades's rule can be seen in a certain kind of obsessive defense. The nit-picking perfectionism practiced by someone like Sula is unconsciously intended to fend off the eruption of Hades into everyday life. A fantasy, in Sula's case directly encouraged by her mother, that bad things happen only because of a broken rule, leads to circular rumination. This rumination is an attempt to discover the rules that will provide the fantasized protection from vulnerability. But of course the rules cannot be found. Hades does not notify us of his fine print, and even the most obsessive, meticulous rule follower will be betrayed eventually. Life will always provide a descent.

The belief that negative or hurtful events are always caused by mistakes or broken rules is problematic not only because it does not work; it also causes blame to rest on both real children and on the Child aspect of the Self. It is an attempt to maintain an identification with the hero persona by denying the existence of innocence itself. Implicating the innocent in his own betrayal, essentially blaming the victim, is often confused with asking the victim to "take responsibility." Victims need to take responsibility for their own transformation but are not responsible for their own betrayal. This is a distinction that can become clearer to us by looking at Demeter's journey.

DEMETER'S JOURNEY:
Confronting and Transforming Betrayal

After Kore's abduction, the myth follows Demeter in her journey, her search for the lost child. The stages of Demeter's quest for Kore, together with the changes caused in Demeter by her quest, give us a pattern for responding to the Divine Child's entrapment in the Underworld. Before Kore's abduction, Demeter is portrayed as a gentle, nurturing soul. She is rarely harsh to human beings and is punitive only when sorely provoked (revealingly her punishments always involve food). She is Demeter Luisa, the nurturing one. Demeter is also innocent and then betrayed, mirroring Kore's experience; Demeter too is her brother's victim. Throughout the myth Demeter's Upperworld experiences provide us with a template for the conscious response to the descent of victimization, while Kore's more-hidden Underworld transformation gives hints of movement in the deep unconscious.

Demeter's first reaction to Kore's disappearance is to search frantically, calling constantly, without eating, drinking, or resting for nine days. She is dressed in deep mourning and appears old, not young and beautiful as she had before the abduction. On the tenth day Demeter goes to Eleusis in disguise and enters into the life of a mortal family. They offer her human comforts for loss and grief: humor, useful work, companionship, understanding. She tries to immortalize Demophoön, an infant son of the house, but fails. Finally, in this human household, her wrath is kindled. She is the only God or Goddess in the Greek pantheon to undergo mourning and loss as mortals do, and in her experience she bridges the separate worlds of the human and the divine. Through her reaction to betrayal the personal and the archetypal are connected.

What is the psychological meaning of these first stages of Demeter's quest for reunion with the Divine Child, Kore? The myth gives us a sense of movement through the experience of loss and betrayal. Demeter's initial helpless, devastated, lonely search must be experienced. In a way, her loss of Kore and their shared betrayal deserves the acknowledgment of those nine days of total immersion in wandering grief. She is consumed by mourning and gives herself completely to this feeling that is hers alone, but she is not consumed forever. Both facets of Demeter's intense loss and longing need to be experienced: the solitary immersion in feeling and the reaching out. She reaches out to a household in which she is accepted and given a useful place. She offers service and is accepted. Eventually, humor reaches her. She takes nourishment and awakens to anger. These are all necessary aspects of her quest, and I suggest that they represent actual acts that one part of the Self must undertake in order to find the abducted Divine Child, another part of the Self, the lost potential trapped in the Underworld.

Many people work hard to avoid the first, full-bodied response of pain and longing for lost innocence. Denial of the betrayal itself is common. Dan, a client who had been singled out by his father for incessant, demeaning criticism, rather desperately maintained that his father's abuse was simply fatherly advice. Dan's unexpressed grief and longing for acceptance roared through his life, unacknowledged and uncomforted, putting him at the mercy of any minor difficulty with an authority figure. Dan was afraid to see his father as a bully, to acknowledge his father's betrayal of Dan's innocent trust, and Dan was afraid of his own feelings, terrified of their lonely intensity.

Such fear is not unreasonable, for it is possible to become stuck at the stage of immersion in loss, experiencing the anorexic response of refusing nourishment both literally in terms of food and metaphorically in terms of joy and connection. The first stage of Demeter's journey reflects a descent into the Underworld of primal loss. The victim can sometimes continue wandering and ceaselessly calling for that which is lost, never reaching out for the connection and sustenance available in the here and now. In this state a person may become saturated, not just with his or her own helpless grief, but by the grief of the world as well. Identification with a deep level of archetypal mourning can turn an individual into a psychic sponge, soaking up the suffering displayed on every street and in every newspaper.

Sula oscillated between these two states on both a daily and a seasonal basis. She would become lost in mourning for past losses and injuries, refusing to eat and withdrawing from the world. Then she would become frightened and try to emerge from grief by denying the reality of the past. This actually made her pain more intense through the added injury of self-abandonment. This occurs when the victim colludes in the denial of her betrayal, leaving the forgotten child alone in the Underworld. The ego takes Zeus's stance and tries to ignore the reality of the betrayal. During these periods of denial, Sula's perfectionism would become relentless and her refusal of food would be experienced as involuntary, through undiagnosable digestive problems. Her grief was expressed unconsciously and somatically.

The loss of innocence, the unfixable nature of past betrayals, and the grief that naturally flows from those betrayals must be consciously accepted, not just unconsciously endured. Mourning responses that are judged illegitimate by the ego of the sufferer do not lead to release. They constitute an unconscious descent. Paradoxically, mourning must be embraced if it is ever to be finished. The archetypal purity, the divine mission of mourning, must then be reconnected to the world of relationships, just as Demeter connects her archetypal Goddess's grief to the mundane world of a family's life. Reaching out to others, the act that can bring dramatic grieving to a close, is extremely difficult in the face of harsh ego judgments, because these internal judgments are often projected outward. In other words, one imagines that others share the ego's lack of acceptance of mourning.

Demeter moves out of her helpless and hopeless state through involving herself with a lively household. She is exposed to and responds to the companionship of the human family. The humor and concern of those around her eventually bring her out of the anorexic depths of despair. She begins to return from her Underworld of loss and betrayal but first attempts to regress. After taking nourishment again Demeter attempts to immortalize the infant prince she is nursing. The fact that this attempt fails and ends in death (another trip to the Underworld) emphasizes the futility of trying to avoid Hades. Once again, and finally, the story demonstrates that one cannot be perfectly protected from loss. Demeter's stay in the household shows that grief and loss can be comforted but not permanently avoided. Descents are inevitable, but return is possible.

Finally Demeter's emergence from despair brings on her wrath. She is now Demeter Erinys, the furious. Her willingness to engage with people leads directly to the person, the swineherd, who has the knowledge she needs. Finally she knows where Kore is, and she is prepared to use her anger and power, confronting authority and pursuing redress. When people feel the wrath of Demeter in themselves it is both a liberating and a devastating experience. The ego comes to full awareness of the betrayal of the innocent child. A part of the Self experiences the Great

Mother's willingness to cause any amount of suffering to others in order to rescue the lost Divine Child. This ruthlessness on behalf of love is absolutely necessary and extremely challenging to handle. It is a ruthless mobilization of all available power and resources to regain connection with the imprisoned Divine Child, with the abducted and exploited innocence, grace, and potential of the Maiden. Demeter is the chthonic power of Earth, emotion, and matter, reaching out at all costs to open a channel to the closed-off Underworld. Demeter undertakes heroic acts without assuming the hero persona; she is not seeking revenge but redress. She exerts strength without denying vulnerability or emotion. And, as we will see, she is open to mediation of her rage.

Demeter never forgets, abandons, or blames Persephone. This is a crucial psychological point. Demeter's stance illuminates a healthy ego attitude. Jung thought that the ego forms a lens or filter that bends external and internal stimuli into shapes it can handle.[11] Consequently, ego consciousness, the ego's attitude toward experience, tends to determine what can be seen and understood. For example, an ego like Sula's has a judgmental and perfectionistic attitude. This means that any external or internal event that can be seen as a flaw to be corrected probably will be seen that way. Seen through the lens of this attitude a victimized child in the unconscious is a flaw, a sign of imperfection, and it must be rejected. In such a case the ego's attitude, its habitual stance, must be brought to awareness and challenged. If the ego consciousness of a person who has been victimized can begin to consciously identify with Demeter, Kore will be transformed into Persephone, who always returns from the Underworld.

There is a strong pull for ego consciousness to identify with either Zeus or Hades, who embody stances that are closer to the cultural norm, more congruent with the heroic ideal. If ego consciousness identifies with Zeus, creating a persona valuing order and the status quo above love for the Divine Child, then Kore is forgotten and the opportunity for transformation is gone too. If ego consciousness identifies with Hades, then the victim will become a victimizer.

It is important that the wrath of Demeter is mediated by Rhea, the mother of Demeter, Zeus, and Hades. Rhea is a daughter of Gaia, and as such she springs from a world order that predates Zeus's domination. She enables Demeter and Zeus, functional opposites in this conflict, to come to a working compromise. Rhea is a mediating mother, one who bridges conflict and who values connection above absolutes. Through her intervention Zeus moves from absolutist domination and Demeter moves from absolutist wrath. The willingness to come out of wrath for a "good enough" resolution is as pivotal as the power of the wrath itself. Rhea enacts a feminine value which is beautifully portrayed by Ibsen in *A Doll's House;* she values relationship over abstract honor and persuades her divine children to do the same.[12] This valuing of connection, whether it is intrinsically or only culturally feminine, is desperately needed by all.

Hecate is also an important mediating figure in the resolution of the myth. Hecate is both an Olympian Goddess and a Titan; like Rhea she is a member of the divine race that predates Zeus's Olympus. She is a remnant, vague but potent, of the old cosmic Goddess of Death and Regeneration in a crone manifestation. Hecate is associated with night, the dark of the moon, with witches, the crossroads, and Cerberus the hound that guards the entrance of the Underworld. In agreeing to watch over and attend to Persephone while she is below, Hecate, as an archaic Mistress of the Dark, may be agreeing to initiate Persephone into her new role as Queen of the Underworld. Hecate aids in reconstituting an older form of the Great Mother Goddess, inclusive of the Dark aspects of the feminine, a form that Zeus's Olympian order ignores. Psychologically Hecate is an image of the part of Self that is comfortable in the unconscious, which pursues intuition and hidden connections outside the light of ego consciousness. She is comfortable at the crossroads between conscious and unconscious knowledge. Hecate enables Persephone to live safely in the Underworld, which is, of course, a key part of Persephone's ability to descend and return. In stories that take place after Persephone becomes Queen of the Underworld she absorbs many of Hecate's attributes. In a way the wholeness of the three-in-one Goddess—Hecate/Demeter/Kore who is Crone/Mother/Maiden—returns through the liminal figure of Persephone.

The gender splits in this myth come to the fore again. Why are all of the mediating figures female? Patriarchal societies like classical Greece, or like our own, tend to divide human attributes and capacities up in particular ways. The capacity to aggressively take what one wants, like Hades, tends to be perceived as masculine, whether it is used positively or negatively. The ability to advocate for a relational approach to problems and to mediate between opposites tends to be perceived as feminine and is embodied in the myth by Rhea and Hecate. These capacities, which are seen as feminine, are necessary to both men and women in the task of transforming victimization. The mediation ability symbolized by Rhea and Hecate is missing in American society's victim debate. Mediation is one aspect of the necessary bridge between opposites that is key to transforming the victim experience.

Attachment to Victim Personae and Hero Personae

The victimization and betrayal of an innocent child lives on in the adult. The Divine Child within, which holds the potential for complete realization of the Self, is split off from the Upperworld of consciousness, enclosed in an unreachable hell with her abductor, refusing to take nourishment, just as Kore and Demeter refuse food during the early stages of their experience. Initially that hell is the unconscious, a personal Underworld in which the child's trauma lives in repressed form together with the part of the Self that identified with the aggressor. When a child is seriously or repeatedly betrayed by an important, trusted adult, a part of the child learns how to betray and abuse from that adult. The adult is teaching the child by modeling betrayal. The abused learn to suffer and learn to abuse at one and the same time. The split between the unconscious Underworld and conscious Upperworld is maintained by personal denial, which is necessary to the survival of a powerless child in overwhelming circumstances, and by the culture's denial of the necessity of a conscious connection to the Underworld. This split, the lack of a bridge between the opposites of Upperworld and Underworld, conscious and unconscious, keeps the Divine Child aspect of the Self in the Underworld. In order to transform this legacy the adult who was betrayed and victimized has to reconnect Underworld and Upperworld. She must refuse the temptation to identify with a hero persona which denies the fact of the victimization and the experience of grief. Zeus and his brother Hades symbolize the light and dark aspects of the hero persona in Persephone's story.

An identification with Zeus's attitude produces a tendency to cling to the orderliness of the split in Self and world, to rationalize the loss and to forget the Child for the sake of the status quo. The adult who clings to this identification is bound to find a way to minimize both his own and everyone else's pain of betrayal, to maintain the fantasy of invulnerability and complete control that characterizes the hero persona. Rationalization and simple avoidance must be used regularly to maintain this stance. This stance is well exemplified by political leaders when they seriously and sincerely state that no child in America goes to sleep hungry. To admit the experience of a starving child is to begin a descent: it requires the feeling loyalty of Demeter's stance, never forgetting the betrayed child. This is a serious challenge to conventional comfort.

An identification with Hades builds on the victim's identification with the aggressor. It is an unacknowledged descent into the unconscious, a flight from the vulnerability of the betrayed child to the rigid perceived strength of the betrayer. In this persona the individual often feels heroic but is seen by others as a force of violent chaos, a self-justifying victimizer engaged in an unconscious replication of abuse. This persona enables members of the Man-Boy Love Association, a group of pedophiles, to explain in detail the good effect they believe they have on the children they molest.[13]

Once the betrayed innocent identifies with Demeter, acknowledging the reality of the loss and remembering the lost Child, there are still three potential psychological pitfalls, three possible victim personae. The first is that the victim may plunge into deep primordial mourning and never emerge. The refusal to accept normal human comforts and reconnect to life may take many forms, though the most dramatic are life-threatening anorexia and bulimia. This victim identity is an endless rumination on the pain of the injury and the irretrievable nature of the loss. Every situation and relationship is infused with the drama of grief. There may be a competitive element, a desire to be acknowledged as bearing the ultimate suffering, being more of a victim than others. This is descent without return, almost a refusal to contemplate the possibility of return. This victim persona is related to Demeter's attempt to immortalize Demophoön, and its underpinning is the same regressive desire to preserve innocence forever.

The second potential pitfall occurs after reconnection brings the extremes of grief to an end; here the problem lies in a resistance to anger and assertion. The desire to retain a super-nice, good-mommy persona and to avoid any possible resemblance, through aggression, to an abuser, leaves the passage to the Underworld of the unconscious closed. Resistance to wrath is particularly strong in women who have been explicitly taught to view power and anger as evil in women (this applies to most women in our culture). Also, the nature of Demeter's wrath threatens the status quo structure of both psyche and society in the most fundamental way. She will stand up to anyone, refusing guilt or rationalization for the sake of the Divine Child. She exerts power. No good-mommy persona can survive this anger, and others will see this. Demeter's anger transforms her before it works any other effects. It is this transformation that is being resisted.

Finally there is a danger in plunging into wrath and becoming addicted to it. This victim identity refuses the good-enough bargain and will not respond to the mediating power of Rhea and Hecate. So Kore never has the chance to become Persephone and the psychological capacities of liminality and tolerance for ambiguity, which are pivotal to the return from victimization, are not developed. Unfortunately, certain kinds of political activism seem to encourage this identification, portraying the search for a good-enough solution as a capitulation. To resist the good-enough solution is to acknowledge the betrayal of innocence but to promote the regressive fantasy that such losses are completely rectifiable if one just holds out long enough: somebody somewhere should have the concrete power to restore my innocence. By keeping a simplistic, black-and-white stance the victim is cut off from the potential inherent in the psychological complexity of victimization.

The myth of Persephone tells us that even a Goddess cannot completely undo what is done. Innocence cannot be recreated, but, once betrayed, must be transmuted into something else. The attitudes and actions of Demeter, Rhea, and Hecate illuminate the psychological capacities that make it possible to deal with the victim's descent and that make a return possible. When, through their intervention, Persephone is revealed as a Goddess who traverses the two worlds, she embodies the archetypal process of bridging the opposites, a process that Jung identifies as fundamental to transcendence.

Bridging the Opposites

The human psyche frequently holds seemingly oppositional aspects like the victim/hero split, like the strictly separated Upperworld and Underworld of this myth. Within our culture's dualistic paradigm, opposites are difficult to tolerate with full awareness. Typically one opposite is favored while the other is ignored. The resulting lack of awareness opens the door to unmediated influence from the unacknowledged opposite. If, however, the opposites of conscious and unconscious, light and shadow (and so on) are in a dialectical relationship—an equal, ongoing dialogue—then consciousness expands to encompass the complementarity of seemingly contradictory realities. The paradoxical nature of some aspects of reality has, in Jung's view, the power to expand consciousness. The dialectic of opposites allows habitual consciousness to be influenced, balanced, and expanded by the rediscovery of lost truths, truths waiting in the unconscious for an opportunity to ascend.

Essentially this is consciousness as process rather than as rigid edifice. Rigid and extreme elements present in either the ego or the unconscious are mediated by the dialectical effect of their opposites. The dialectical effect of the symbolic dialogue between the unconscious (Underworld) and conscious (Upperworld) aspects of the Self is fundamental. The dialogue between conscious and unconscious parts of the Self is a cycle of descent and return, causing the ego to examine the limits of its consciousness, exposing those limits to the continuously modifying effects of dialogue. The dialogue with motifs welling up from within the unconscious and with the subjective truth of other peoples' stories profoundly affects the ego's attitude, stance, and use of personae. Attempts to consciously hold opposites that arise in relationship to the victim experience can protect the ego from identifying with a particular persona. An example of this arose in Sula's psychotherapy when she was able to recognize her sadistic desire to have revenge on her boss while simultaneously feeling her legitimate sense of being exploited and victimized by that same boss. Consciousness of both the self-righteous hero response and the overwhelmed victim response caused a fruitful tension in Sula, expanding both her sense of herself and her sense of her boss as a fellow human being.

Once the ego becomes aware of the part of Self that is trapped in the Underworld, abandoned in the unconscious through denial and rationalization, it can begin Demeter's journey: allowing the deep grief, then reconnecting to wholesome relationships that acknowledge and comfort the grief, followed by increased awareness of the nature of the loss, then wrath and, finally, acceptance of the good-enough resolution of betrayal. The ego must be alert for the pitfalls of identifying with Zeus's or Hades's stance and open to the mediating qualities of Rhea and Hecate. This brings ego consciousness into communication with the unconscious, and a Persephone-like liminality bridges Upperworld and Underworld within the Self. The Underworld of the unconscious holds the transformative potential inherent in the descent/ascent cycle, the potential that has lost its cultural place, the potential embodied in the figure of Persephone who traverses the opposites of Upperworld and Underworld.

The psychological capacity symbolized by Persephone's eternal cycle of ascent and descent is multifaceted; it is the personal and transpersonal capacity for liminality. Liminal literally means "of the threshold"; in this case the threshold is between the conscious and unconscious, the personal and the transpersonal, Upperworld and Underworld. The willingness to enter a liminal state and to be affected by symbolic communication from within is the gateway to the transpersonal dimension of the Self. Liminality was originally defined in anthropological literature as an aspect of initiation rituals or rites of passage. A rite of passage incorporates three stages for the initiate: (1) detachment from a fixed social structure and identity; (2) entering a threshold state of ambiguity (liminality); (3) resolution into a new, very different identity. Liminality is a "condition of ambiguity and paradox, a confusion of customary categories . . . and a realm of pure possibility,"[14] a condition that makes initiation into a new state of being possible. Strikingly and significantly, Persephone's rite of passage is resolved through an incorporation of the liminal state into her new identity as Queen of the Underworld. Her new identity is a liminal one, one that confuses customary categories, and thus her image and her story become a gateway for the initiation of others. The liminal tolerance for ambiguity allows us to hold the opposite truths of the hero ideal and the victim ideal without beatifying or demonizing.

"Liminality breaks the cake of custom and enfranchises speculation."[15] Speculation, reflection, fluidity, and symbolic thinking are all enfranchised by the liminal image of Persephone. Psychologically the liminal state is one of connection and communication between conscious and unconscious aspects of the psyche, and the unconscious includes the transpersonal resources of the collective unconscious. Jungian theorists have discussed the psychological processes that both produce and spring from the liminal state as "mediality." Beginning with Toni Wolff, mediality has been portrayed as a property of the feminine, as in "the medial woman" who connects the conscious to the unconscious.[16] Persephone is certainly a mediatrix, but is this an exclusively female capacity?

In fact liminality and mediality occur frequently. "Man or woman we are all medial to some degree."[17] However, the common modes of information and perception in the liminal or medial state—such as emotion, intuition, somatic sensation, fantasy, metaphorical association, visualization, and imagination—are all sources of perception and knowledge to which women have had a special cultural connection. Whether that connection is somehow an intrinsic part of being a woman or whether it is the result of woman's position as shadow carriers in patriarchal society is a much-debated issue. In any case these ways of knowing, associated with women and with feminine imagery, have been trivialized and pathologized by the culturally dominant hyper-rational approach to knowledge. The tendency to stigmatize all "nonrational" forms of knowing and to associate them with disenfranchised social groups has given all noncognitive modes of perception an uneasy, feminized epistemological status. The pain and shame that come from identifying one's own deep, inarticulate, inchoate perceptions as crazy contributes to a typical ego attitude that tends to ignore the value of the liminal state.

The willingness to accept and value the knowledge and experience, the potential inherent in the liminal state, in the connection to the Underworld, depends on the ego's attitude. An ego that is identified with either the hero ideal or the victim ideal will filter symbolic communications through the lens of a distorting attitude. The ego will then be closed to the compensating, balancing communications of the unconscious. The compensatory purpose of the unconscious is to balance and regenerate consciousness by communicating denied aspects of the Self and the world to the dominant ego. Thus the unconscious functions as a storehouse of forgotten resources, an Underworld of potential transformations, which it communicates through the medium of the symbol.

The forms of symbolic communication between conscious and unconscious aspects of the Self are myriad. Images and narratives encountered in dreams, trance states (however induced), and states of reverie, such as daydream, are the most obvious symbolic products of the unconscious. Unconscious material is also woven throughout the warp of everyday, workaday life. The experience of inexplicable revulsions and allurements, gripping moods and body states that appear to have little or no basis in external events, compulsive behaviors, seemingly random thought streams, intense responses to people—any or all such experiences may spring from the unconscious. If the ego, the everyday consciousness, of the victim can turn toward these symbolic communications, then the transformative power of the unconscious is available to him or her. The betrayal of innocence is an initiation into the Underworld, and the myth of Persephone's rape and transformation illuminates the new psychological capacity possible for the initiate.

According to Helene Foley, a classics scholar, the story of Persephone and Demeter, together with the Eleusinian Mystery rites that derive from and enact the myth, constitute a "psychological reality so powerful that it can transcend death and the limits of the universe."[18] That psychological reality is the capacity to enter into and tolerate a liminal transformative state that bridges opposites. The victim whose innocence is betrayed can use the story of Demeter and Persephone as an imaginal guide to the recovery of liminality, embodied by Persephone. That liminal capacity survived the patriarchal Greek worldview in the form of the Eleusinian Mysteries; those rites served as the container. However, the modern Western individual must find and maintain a container for the development of this key psychological ability, an ability which allows access to the storehouse of transformative images in the unconscious. Working with stories that touch the archetypal level, such as myths and fairy tales, develops this liminal capacity. Explorations of symbol and narrative like those in the following chapters help to bridge Upperworld and Underworld experience, conscious and unconscious aspects of the Self. Image and narrative begin to build the necessary container for holding seeming opposites in consciousness and allowing symbolic dialogue between them.

The story of Persephone is a "great myth." As such it is a metastory, giving us an overview of a profound personal and cosmological process. A great myth of descent and return portrays the universal underpinnings, the deep structure, as it were, of a common human experience and, as a consequence, such a myth illuminates the numinous meaning of that experience. However, because of this depth, such a myth tends to use imagery that is somewhat distant from daily human life. On the other hand fairy tales seem to be "built up from inner experiences" embodying more detailed, everyday human experiences that do not exactly fit the more sweeping images of a great cosmological myth.[19] The following chapters use fairy tales rather than myths to explicate specific victim personae. A fairy tale is an archetypal story that can mediate between the "otherness" of mythic images and everyday life; it is a mixture of the mundane and the mythic. In a sense the myth of Persephone gives us the fundamental form of the victim's journey of descent and return. But in life there are particular kinds of descents, specific ways in which the Divine Child aspect of the Self is dragged down into the Underworld. These necessitate particular forms of Demeter-consciousness and specific kinds of mediation that make a return possible. The following chapters, based on the connections between various victim experiences and various fairy tales, clothe the fundamental form of descent and return in the specifics of human experience.

CHAPTER THREE

VICTIM AS REDEEMER

Beauty and the Beast

A RICH merchant had three daughters. The two oldest were vain, selfish, and jealous of the youngest, Beauty, who was not only beautiful but also modest, charming, and helpful to everyone. The merchant, having trusted unfaithful clerks, suddenly lost all his wealth. The family's friends, thinking that their misfortune sprang from their self-indulgence, would not help them. The family had no savings and fell into direst poverty. Beauty tried to make the best of things, to help her father and remain cheerful. The merchant heard that one of his ships might have survived and decided to go away in an attempt to regain some of his fortune. The two oldest sisters demanded that he return with expensive presents for them; Beauty modestly asked her father only for a rose.

Returning from his unsuccessful venture, he got lost in a forest during a snowstorm. He spent the first night in a hollow tree and he feared he would perish on the second, but then he came upon a palace. No snow was falling on this estate; indeed it was in bloom and warm. He slept in a prepared room and ate elaborate meals, but the servants were invisible. The next morning the merchant saw some beautiful roses and picked one for Beauty. As he did so, a hideous beast appeared and roared,"This is the way you show your gratitude—by stealing my flowers!"

"I beg you to forgive me," the merchant said, "for I meant no harm." The Beast considered for a moment and said, "I will forgive you if you give me one of your daughters. If they will not come, you will belong to me!"

The merchant returned home, gave Beauty the rose, and told her what happened. She returned with him to the magic palace, and the Beast, making sure she had come of her own free will, told her father to leave, taking with him two traveling trunks filled with everything Beauty's siblings might like to have.

The Beast wooed Beauty and granted all her wishes. She received marvelous dresses. The palace contained every musical instrument she ever wanted to play, every book she ever wanted to read. The magical palace supplied beautiful distractions and perfect comfort. She grew accustomed to the Beast's hideousness. Every evening after supper the Beast came to see her and asked in his terrible voice, "Beauty, will you marry me?" and when she said, "No, Beast," it seemed that he went away quite sad.

One day while looking in the magic mirror she saw her ailing father pining for her. The Beast gave her a week's time to go home but warned her that he himself would die if she failed to return. At home, Beauty's greedy sisters, envious of her fine clothes and rich possessions, plotted to detain Beauty in hopes that the Beast would destroy her in a fury. She stayed on and on. On the tenth night, however, Beauty saw the Beast in a dream. He was reproaching her in a dying voice. She sped back to find him near death. Overwhelmed with grief, she said, "I never knew how much I loved you until now."

At this the Beast turned into a handsome prince. He had been under the spell of a witch and could resume his true form only if a girl could love and marry him despite his hideousness. At their wedding her sisters were changed into statues, having to silently witness Beauty's happiness, to be human again only if they owned up to their faults.[1]

Nature and Development of the Redeemer Identity

Beauty and the Beast presents us with a particular victim persona, one in which the "sins" of an entire family are taken on by the most competent, appealing, and talented member of the family, who then tries to redeem those sins. This dynamic is in sharp contrast to scapegoat stories like "Cinderella," in which the family projects its collective shadow onto a despised outcast who, as a consequence, lives a degraded life. Instead we find that Beauty lives what appears to be a fulfilling life, in which she is admired and envied. Unlike Cinderella or Manypelts (the protagonist of the fairy tale in chapter 5) the deprivations Beauty suffers seem to be entirely of her own choosing and tend to display her virtue.

The Redeemer victim identity is very common in women, and, since the protagonists of both the fairy tale and the main case history used here are women, it may seem that I am describing a situation that is uniquely female. Some aspects of the Beauty role do have a strong relationship to the feminine gender role in Western culture, a relationship that will be discussed toward the end of this chapter. However, men may also become identified with this victim persona.

The story is explicit concerning Beauty's intention in playing her sacrificial role: she is protecting her father from the consequences of his own acts. By asking for a single rose she is careful not to ask him to provide much, since he is a poor provider, showing questionable judgment in business and in budgeting the family's resources. When her father has a dangerous experience with the Beast (brought on by his poor judgment in traveling unprepared during a snowstorm and in tampering with an obviously enchanted place), Beauty steps in to bear the consequences of her father's choices.

These acts, undertaken to redeem her father's ineptness and bad luck, cause her to inherit his sins, as it were, to take on the responsibility for working out his fate. In addition to the deprivations of unnecessary poverty, Beauty's family also suffers from the stigma and pressure of her sisters' selfish shallowness and demanding materialism. No one in the family confronts the sisters' destructive and repugnant behavior. Instead, Beauty tries to compensate for it through her equally extreme purity and self-sacrifice. This systemic counterbalancing of roles is very familiar to family therapists, and it resonates with the dynamics of demonization and beatification that suffuse the victim discourse. Ultimately Beauty provides the riches her sisters crave through giving herself to the Beast, even though meeting the sisters' unrelenting demands has, in part, led to the family's downfall. Beauty, however, is not a betrayed innocent dragged down against her will but a willing victim who seems to choose entrapment. She is not a bereft stepchild abandoned in the cinders. She is a wonder child meant to redeem the family deficits, to tame its beast. And yet Beauty is as much a scapegoat as any Cinderella; her voluntary entrapment with her demonic companion is as real as Persephone's involuntary entrapment with the King of Hell.

Beauty's Relationship to the Beast

The magical and abundant material benefits of Beauty's life with the Beast help us picture the seductiveness of this particular victim identity and its ambiguous rewards. The talented child who is chosen (and, as an adult, continues to choose) to take on the family's sins as a Redeemer comes into a peculiarly ambivalent relationship to the family's "Beast." In this relationship Beauty bears the brunt of the beastliness in classic scapegoat fashion, but, unlike the usual scapegoat, she is also elevated over other family members, perceived by all as very special. She acts out a subtle form of the hero persona, in which her fundamental vulnerability and need are masked by perfectionism. It is the denial of these basic human traits that allows Beauty to form a relationship to the Beast that traps her in a victim position. The extremes of her hero persona flip over into a victim identity.

The family Beast may be alcoholism or other addictions, material failure, debilitating depression, abuse, or simple, chronic unhappiness; it may be manifest in one person's behavior or be shared by several family members. In any case, the family's Beauty takes on a closely identified connection with the family's Beast, in which she endures, admonishes, contains, and soothes its beastliness. This willingness to take on the Beast relieves the other members of the family from the task of consciously relating to and grappling with the toxic aspects of their collective life, although they are still unconsciously affected by those aspects. Beauty's special relationship to the family Beast is intrinsic to the way in which such a family maintains its systemic denial. In essence the family group has a persona figure, Beauty, and a shadow figure, the Beast, who balance each other out.

What does the special relationship do to Beauty? Jane, the client spoken of in the introduction, took on a Redeemer identity in her family. Alcoholism, with its attendant psychological deformity of massive denial, was the Beast in her family. It first manifested in her father's sadistic tantrums and overwhelming domination of his children's lives. After his death, when Jane was a young teenager, the family Beast returned in the form of Jane's mother's complete drunken withdrawal from parental responsibility. The fairy tale separates the role of the hapless family members who need to be saved from that of the explicit Beast (who also needs to be saved), but in Jane's family, as in most, the same people played both parts. In Jane's childhood and adulthood her parents and her brother were alternately incompetent family members desperate for financial and spiritual rescue and hideous, abusive Beasts from whom there was no escape. This unpredictable inconsistency is common in, but not exclusive to, alcoholic families. Jane's father, mother, and brother were all people with more than one aspect to their personalities. Some aspects invoked compassion and love, while some invoked fear and loathing. This is normal and true for all families, for all human beings. However, the pathology of the family, especially the dynamics of alcoholism, meant that the fearsome or beastly aspects of personality ran unchecked and unacknowledged by the adults in the family. Jane was fundamentally alone in her attempts to deal with the family's shadow or Beast.

Jane took the family's Beast on in many ways: including developing aspects of herself that were like her father so as to be strong enough to engage and distract him, and honing a preternatural ability to observe and predict capricious adult behavior. If these strategies failed, she protected her younger siblings by bearing the brunt of brutal beatings. She took on her mother's duties after alcoholism rendered her mother incompetent. She struggled for achievements that would rectify the family's stature in the community, particularly as her mother's incapacity became more and more public. All of Jane's efforts to be redeemingly perfect could not rectify the family's fundamental problems, just as Beauty's efforts do not change her father or sisters. The adults in the family continued to indulge in and deny the effects of alcoholism, violence, and bad judgment. Jane was left to deal with the Beast alone, as Beauty is left alone in the enchanted palace.

The terrible loneliness and fear of this role is illustrated by a dream that Jane had when she was nine. In the dream a sorcerer-dentist intended to kill her in order to save her family. Her parents and siblings all agreed to this plan and she knew she had no option. This dream portrays for us in no uncertain terms the inner strain, terror, and withering effect of the Redeemer victim identity. As is said in Alcoholics Anonymous, alcoholics don't have relationships, they take hostages. Jane and Beauty are both held hostage for their families' unaddressed problems and particularly for their fathers' unacknowledged faults.

Jane was the star of her family—intelligent, articulate, responsible, artistic, high-achieving. Her younger siblings were alternately scorned and infantilized by her parents, aunts, and uncles. The younger children were, in the family ethos, demeaned yet privileged by their position as real children needing real care. They received little or no respect and admiration, but they were expected to be children and consequently had a freedom that was unavailable to Jane. Jane's identity as the child who was more effectively adult than the family's adults appeared to give her many rewards, ranging from the trivial to the substantial. Her precocious skills, developed in the desperate context of rescuing the family, served her in many ways. She had better clothes because she taught herself to sew. She had the respect of the adults. She excelled at school, eventually winning a scholarship. Her siblings achieved little. It seemed outwardly that her strivings for perfection and her special relationship to the Beast in the family had strengthened her, helped her find a better fate. It seemed outwardly that she might manage to redeem the family through her constant strivings.

But Jane's childhood dream and the fairy tale both portray the hidden price of identifying with the Beauty persona. While Beauty is with her family, her talents, energy, and spirit are devoted to counterbalancing their self-indulgences and bad judgments. When this self-sacrifice leads to her imprisonment at the palace of the Beast, she appears to be rewarded by material wealth and comfort. But the reality of her situation is that she has saved her father and enriched her family by giving up all freedom and choice. Her identity, by which I mean her image of herself and her sense of purpose, meaning, and direction in the world, now centers around expiating, through self-sacrifice, her father's real and imagined transgressions. She has descended into the Underworld of the Beast and has no option but to accustom herself to the Beast's hideousness and be grateful for any gentleness she happens to find. As in Jane's dream of dying for the family's well-being, there is no option, no opportunity, to allow life to unfold an individual destiny. In a culture obsessed by material values it can be difficult to empathize with or even fully recognize the damage being done to the life of a person who is identified with the Redeemer victim identity. The palace is beautiful, abundant with fascinating objects, but it is as much a trap as Persephone's Underworld, a world in which personal choice and the possibility of an individual destiny are nonexistent. The potential for a unique wholeness, the chance to develop the Self, is lost in the Underworld, just as Kore was lost.

The Enchanted Palace

Beauty's entrapment in the palace of the Beast reflects the simple reality of the child's lack of choice in the family situation. The reality of entrapment is carried forward to adult life in internal and external forms. The Redeemer persona requires that one become accustomed to hideousness. One must come to treat beastliness as familiar and ignore its possible dangers. This rather sinister habit, combined with a self-image that depends absolutely on redeeming others, leads to intimate relationships that recreate the exploitive family. In young adulthood Jane had several relationships in which she struggled to redeem dangerously violent men and was at least once in danger of losing her life to a loved one.

Jane also excelled at working for alcoholic, marginal bosses, constantly saving the day without regard to her own needs, making herself indispensable. She gained many material rewards in her work. She was widely admired but experienced little or no joy, pride, choice, or peace in the process. Her perfect service was compulsive, and the rewards could rarely be enjoyed. Jane continued to try to redeem the fate of her original family members by continually getting them out of various financial, legal, and emotional jams (once again without regard to the effect on her own life). She regularly became attached to new people, at work and in her personal life, who harbored Beasts similar to the family's and who also required saving.

The invisible servants of the story, who perform vital tasks perfectly without being seen, evoke the way in which the talents of the person identified with the Redeemer persona are used without self-recognition, pride, or joy. It is necessary to be very competent in order to fully compensate for the deficiencies of the Beasts who need to be redeemed. At the same time it is necessary to efface competence and talents in order to preserve the reputation of the family, lover, or boss who is being saved and to preserve the image of selfless purity. The normal human enjoyments of praise or joy in achievement are out of bounds to the Redeemer. The fruits of effort belong to the project of redemption, not to the Self.

Jane had also been in love, in her twenties, with a non-abusive man. However, when he would not allow her to sacrifice for him, she assumed that his love was not real. She left him. Jane's identification with the Redeemer persona had made love synonymous with the complete sacrifice of self, with the offering of constant work and accommodation to the beloved, with the project of saving the incompetent and/or terrifying love object. A competent partner, offering a relationship of parity, could not evoke a sense of intimacy, nor could a nonexploitive lover save her from the power of her internal identification with compulsive self-sacrifice.

In her sacrifice of choice and development, Beauty is simultaneously a victim and a redeemer. She redeems others by striving to be pristine, selfless, pure, and perfect. Unlike typical heroes, who roam the wide world in search of their destiny, Beauty is caught within a confined space, symbolized by the magic palace. Within that confined space her life is defined by the interaction of polar opposites; extremes of selfless perfection oppose voracious beastliness. These two poles are defined by and embodied in herself and the Beast. Through looking at Jane's life we have explored the ways in which these polar opposites dominate the Redeemer's life in the family, in adult relationships, and in the workplace. In her connection to out-of-control family members, incompetent bosses and violent lovers, Jane personified and lived the perfectionistic, sacrificing role, while her various partners played out the opposite, the Beast. In a more subtle and insidious way the same opposites dominate the inner life of the psyche.

The internal world of a person who identifies with the Redeemer persona resembles the Beast's estate and incorporates its denizens. Inner life is isolated, cut off from the world, unchanged since childhood, just as the enchanted estate is unaffected by time, season and weather. Internal reflective space, which springs from the capacity to observe, consider, assess, and understand one's inner process with interest and some objectivity (as opposed to compulsivity) is necessary for the experience of choice. Internal space is not free or reflective for the Redeemer but is instead a prison of prescribed thoughts and imperative roles within which the impossibly perfect Beauty and the impossibly hideous Beast both live. An outer identification with Beauty is accompanied by an internalization of the Beast as shadow. The demonization and beatification processes seen in the cultural arena operate within the Redeemer's psyche. Inner life is controlled by the constant tension between these internalized polar opposites, a tension characterized by black-and-white moral judgments, compulsive thoughts, and unmediated waves of anxiety. The "capacity to develop an inside, to be a container,"[2] cannot develop in this context; the liminal capacity for bridging the opposites, Persephone's mediality, is not available. The Beast's enchanted estate is an Underworld in which the potential of Beauty's developing Self, the spark of the Divine Child in her, is trapped. However, in coming to terms with the Beast she is eventually able to use this seeming trap as an external container that helps her to individuate. In order to understand the psychological significance of the Beast, we must continue the discussion of the interaction between family dynamics and the child's development of an internal sense of self.

The Shadow-Beast

In the child's special relationship with the family Beast she not only incorporates the unreachably high standards of Beauty, but she also internalizes the Beast. A child must identify with the adults in the family in order to form a sense of self. In Jane's family Jane had to identify with the same people who manifested beastliness in her everyday life. This produced a special form of closeness that allowed her to understand and deal with the Beast most effectively. This ability to grasp the hidden qualities of another person is one of the Redeemer's talents, the magic mirror with which she can perceive the needs of those she must redeem. In the enclosed world of Jane's family her role required that she be simultaneously very different from her father and very like him. In order to keep the peace and provide her siblings with stability she had to be responsible, even-tempered, and self-controlled, as her father was not. In order to feel powerful enough to be the Redeemer and in order to influence her father, she had to be tough, driven, and articulate, as he was. The child who is Redeemer-identified takes the normal parent-child dynamics of identification and internalization and intensifies them in order to more effectively perform her role of understanding and handling the Beast for her family. This gives her the intensified perceptions and intuitions she needs to redeem the family, and it helps produce a hidden shadow-Beast that compensates the outer perfectionistic Redeemer persona.

The desperate need for redemption in the family creates a climate in which normal temperamental inclinations toward altruism and perfectionism are experienced as the only good parts of the Self, forming the basis of the persona, the Redeemer identification. Normal aggression and human imperfections become evil internal threats, associated with the beastly behavior of out-of-control family members, forming the basis of a demonized shadow aspect of the personality. The perfectionism demanded by the Redeemer identity requires that many ordinary impulses and aspects of the Self be split off from everyday awareness, repressed, and suppressed. The shadow created by this splitting is very large and threatening. These disparate parts of the Self have scant, and chiefly adversarial, connection. The tyranny of the extreme opposites at work here creates a split, black-and-white perception of self and world, leaving a deep chasm between persona and shadow.

The internal shadow-Beast may be consciously perceived. Jane was aware of hers from the age of six, calling it the Evil Twin. The Evil Twin once vandalized a house; it/she preferred to do things that would enrage Jane's father if he ever discovered them. This both terrified and enthralled Jane, much as the Beast both terrifies and enthralls Beauty. In adulthood the Evil Twin took a secret pleasure in the humiliation of Jane's business rivals, a pleasure that Jane judged to be entirely "creepy." Sometimes the Redeemer-identified person does not clearly perceive an internal beastly shadow aspect. In that case he or she experiences it instead as loathing for a dissociated part of the self. The process of dissociation allows the ego to maintain its identification with the perfectionistic Redeemer identity while relating to another part of the Self as Beast. Often, in women, the body or a specific body part will take on the aura of the shadow-Beast. However, this dynamic can attach to almost any facet of the Self in men and women; such normal aspects as speech, sexual desire, desire for recognition, or assertiveness can be made beastly through the process of dissociation.

The Redeemer victim identity often produces hyper-vigilance concerning flaws in others. Perceiving the Beast by projecting the inner shadow onto others reassures the ego of its comparative perfection and creates foci for the exercise of redemptive sacrifice. The cultivation of selfless perfection and indispensability is, in Western culture, a peculiarly feminine style of saving others. It is not exclusive to women, but as an avenue for the hidden expression of power and specialness it is common in groups of people who have little access to direct power and status and who must therefore find indirect expression for their normal aggressive drives. The Redeemer persona allows one to express considerable underground aggression and competition. This aggression commonly emerges as an intense scrutiny of others and a hyper-awareness of their flaws. Under the cover of helpfulness, a kind of scorn for those being helped may develop. The intensity of self-sacrifice is often matched by an unspoken intensity of contempt, an indirect, shadowy expression of normal crankiness, which is outlawed by the selfless persona. The nagging, bitchy, angry sisters of the fairy tale also live in the repressed unconscious of the Redeemer. There is a noticeable lack of mediation between parts of the Self, little sense of a good-enough solution between conflicting aspects of inner experience.

No matter how many outer Beasts Beauty saves, she carries her own Beast within, always seeking to redeem its beastliness through ever more perfect behavior and sacrifice. The driven, energy-consuming nature of her perfectionism mitigates against the kind of insight and self-reflection that might lead to facing and redeeming her own internal shadow-Beast. The ability to "hold oneself, to bear one's feelings without losing or fragmenting oneself—an ability crucial to introspection and self-discovery"[3]—is not available. The normal human imperfections Beauty sees in herself and in those to whom she is close, cannot be the focus of "introspection and self-discovery" but rather are indications of the secretly carried Beast within and are therefore horrifying. Flaws in oneself or in others are framed in moralistic and judgmental language. The inevitable flaws that emerge in everyday life cannot be experienced as ordinary obstacles. Instead they are threatening signs of imperfection, and she must work ever harder to eradicate them, pursuing the fantasy that perfection is attainable and will redeem the Beast, both in others and as it is experienced within. But the shadow-Beast's hideousness is not eradicated by any achievement, any perfection of behavior or self.

Attachment to the Victim Identity

An important turning point in the fairy tale depicts Beauty's return to her family. Beauty rushes once more into the role of self-sacrificing savior to her father. Once again she does nothing direct to protect herself from the toxic intentions of her sisters. Nothing appears to have changed in the family or in Beauty. This episode in the fairy tale highlights the issue of loyalty. Beauty's return to and length of stay with her family members is completely determined by their needs. She does not consider her own needs or the Beast's. The Redeemer's loyalty is to the family she must redeem (or to their later stand-ins), to her internalized role of Redeemer, and to the lifelong project of eliminating or at least totally containing the shadow-Beast within. Loyalty to the Self, to the potential of the Divine Child within, and to the Self's preferences, talents, freedom, or development is not only minimal but usually unimaginable.

Why do people continue to choose attachments and circumstances that work to keep them entrapped? The child's original choice of loyalty to the family is inevitable, a matter of survival, and takes place in a pressured family context. The adult's continued re-creation of and attachment to the Redeemer persona may need further explication. In describing the continuous re-creation, in adults, of relationships and situations that support and encourage the victim identification that began in childhood, I have not explicitly addressed the question of choice. This question is particularly pressing with the Redeemer. Individuals like Jane have plenty of character, willpower, and ability. The accusations of victim backlash commentators, citing general weakness, dependency, and lack of moral fiber as the prime determinants of victim "character," clearly do not apply in such cases. Why do such strong and talented individuals still exhibit limited judgment in choosing personal relationships?

As we have already discussed, the internal effects of compulsively performing the Redeemer role leave little room for self-reflection or for the experience of choice, which can spring from such reflection. A life-and-death pressure to act rather than reflect and choose often attaches to the project of redeeming others. This pressure to act rather than reflect, which we have also noted on the collective, societal level, springs from two sources. Historically the life-threatening incompetence and violence of the adults in the family of origin made it necessary to act quickly, often in an adrenaline rush, and made it unbearably painful to reflect much on events. In adulthood an internal feeling of deathly emptiness, which is fed by compulsive attention to others, prompts the desire to "fill up" with projects and tasks. This withering neglect of the Self feels desperate and life-threatening, but it is addressed only through sacrifice to others.

I am not trying to imply here that caring for others is not fulfilling. Giving can be extremely nurturing to the giver, when giving is freely chosen and its limits are clearly seen. When giving is choiceless and desperate, it becomes a joyless task that never yields the hoped-for product of inner fulfillment. The pressure to give and redeem can overwhelm impulses to reflect, choose, and seek guidance from within, just as Beauty's growing relationship to the Beast is overwhelmed by the intrusion of her family's latest crisis.

A very different aspect of an adult's attachment to the Redeemer persona lies in the heroic glory that attends its successes. It is common for the perfectionism and selflessness that accompany a Redeemer identification to draw tremendous admiration and dependency from others. The Redeemer persona can feel like an aura of specialness and power, even though the power is frequently indirectly expressed. As such it can be addictive, making it hard for the Redeemer-identified person to imagine and accept being more "ordinary." Identification with the Redeemer persona makes it hard to conceptualize a human specialness based on the unique qualities of the inner Self rather than on perfection and indispensability. Consequently the sisters in the tale find it easy to convince Beauty that she is indispensable, and she finds it impossible to tap into the inner guidance that would be necessary to counteract their machinations. The internalized nagging demand to be indispensable, to redeem the faults of loved ones, and to resist separation from partners who need redemption interrupts attempts to reflect on and connect to the Self, to the Self's denied aspects, to the shadow, the internal Beast. The capacity to bridge these internal opposites, to allow a liminal approach to the unconscious, must be developed.

Help from the Unconscious

It is important that a dream gives Beauty the strength to finally break from her family's constant demands and from her own role in the family system. The ability and willingness to seriously attend to a dream, to act on the communication of a dream, requires an internal reflective space that can be hard-won. The individual experiences a circular impasse in which attaining a necessary condition for internal transformation—an internal reflective space—itself requires a transformative shift. Frequently that shift is inspired by a symbolic experience, a nudge from the unconscious: a dream, a synchronous event, or a work of art might break the impasse. This is possible because the unconscious holds a compensating, balancing drive to rectify the imbalances of the ego. The compensatory purpose of the unconscious is to balance and regenerate consciousness by communicating, via symbolic dialogue, denied aspects of the Self and of experience to the ego. Thus the unconscious functions as a storehouse of forgotten resources which it communicates through the medium of symbolic dialogue. A connection to the Underworld of the unconscious can be indispensable to the process of transforming the Redeemer persona.

Late in the course of therapy, Jane began to take art classes, reconnecting to a childhood aspiration that had been left behind. About this time she had a dream in which an assignment for a photography class led her to a cave. The front of the cave held images of abuse and perversity; the middle of the cave was a pool of water in which creatures transformed. The back of the cave was a studio in which Jane was able to produce a wonderful photograph of a man and woman in spiritual union. As this dream vividly illustrates, the experience of gaining access to the unconscious is not like opening an ordered storehouse and selecting a transformative resource but rather like plunging into a tangle of interwoven images and feelings. Repressed pathogens, aspects of the shadow like those portrayed in the cave entrance, intersect with unrealized spiritual potentials, symbolized in the pool of water and art studio, interlocking in ways that can be profoundly confusing and sometimes dangerous. What makes it possible to connect to the helpful, change-inducing aspects of the unconscious?

The Necessary Container

Successful access to the transformative power of the unconscious requires an adequate container. The container must be sturdy enough to withstand the chaos of regeneration. In Jane's case, intensive individual psychotherapy provided a container. In fact, the concept of the container, as used here, springs from the practice of depth psychotherapy. Various names are used in that practice—container, *temenos,* holding function, frame—to denote a bounded, some would say sacred, space within the therapeutic relationship, a space that is needed for the developing internal reflective space. In essence, the nature of the external relationship between therapist and client eventually becomes internalized for the client as a model for relationships between aspects of the self. The internalized container, in Jane's dream symbolized by the cave itself, holds the rich chaos of conscious and unconscious experience; it allows a multitude of fragmentary images to be sorted out and deeply felt, to interrelate and be held in consciousness; it provides a framework for bridging the split between victim identity and shadow, enabling conscious delineation of the pathological aspects from the enriching potentials of the unconscious. The need to actively build and nurture such a container, whether in therapy or out, is particularly pressing for an individual who has been conditioned to distrust inner perceptions in favor of the victim identity.

Psychotherapy that is oriented toward self-reflection rather than immediate symptom reduction is most helpful. Therapeutic approaches that present the Self as a remodeling project foster perfectionism and will probably reinforce this form of victim identification. Ironically, the Redeemer persona may predispose an individual toward just those therapeutic interventions that promise a quick fix, fast freedom from the necessity of dealing with the shadow at all. Such approaches will reinforce the fantasy of perfectionism. Psychotherapies that depend on the development of a healing relationship with the therapist will be most helpful.

Can the process of building a container occur outside of therapy? The development of the container, as an inner structure holding reflective space, depends on nonexploitive relationships that do not re-create the family pattern, relationships in which relationship partners do not need someone to inherit their sins, do not need to be redeemed. Such relationships must have a place for the shadow-Beast, an interpersonal dynamic that does not require hiding or instantly fixing the shadow. The relationships that nurture the container must actively support a shift in ego stance within the individual. The ego's task in the process of making such a container is not its usual one of analysis, judgment, categorization, and control. Instead, the ego shifts, using a more observing, empathetic, aesthetic, and perhaps feminine stance, which allows all stories to be told, to complement one another, until a picture of the personal myth is built up.

Twelve-step programs, when properly conducted, provide nonexploitive, supportive group and individual relationships. Such programs as AA, NA, and Al-Anon have a built-in structure for long-term self-reflection. That structure—the steps, the form of the meetings, and the sponsor relationship—fosters awareness of the problems inherent in redeeming others and can be an excellent container for those who are attached to the Redeemer persona. It is important that the steps are actually worked and that the sponsor is adequately neutral. Simple attendance of meetings without "working the program" will not be effective.

Spiritual communities that rigorously avoid any exploitation of disciples may also provide the relationships necessary for the development of a container and the consequent development of a new attitude toward the Self. Spiritual communities in which disciples are encouraged to place the leader's well-being or the community's pragmatic goals above their own spiritual practice will not be helpful.

I know of few instances in which an individual has made the required shift in ego stance by herself, without the help of nurturing relationships. In her book *An Unknown Woman,* Alice Koller describes a rigorous, solitary process of self-examination by which she radically changed her attitude toward herself and her life.[4] She managed to create and maintain a container that allowed the Self to emerge and to begin to influence the ego (she does not use Jungian terms to describe the process). Anyone wishing to follow a similar path will find her work inspiring.

In the fairy tale, Beauty's voluntary return to the enchanted palace and her acceptance of the Beast symbolize the internalization of a container for self-exploration. She is no longer trapped by her father's actions in a bizarre Underworld but is able to come and go to a special place in which she has, finally, chosen a new kind of relationship to the Beast. In a similar way, the inner world of the Redeemer can go from being a frightening trap filled with the compulsions developed in an exploitive family life to a private, transformative world explored through choice.

Transformation

Returning to the fairy tale we can see Beauty's attention to her dream and to her realization of her own feelings instead of to her family's demands as evidence of her developing an internal container that allows for reflection on her own needs and preferences. This paves the way for her union with the Beast. The marriage of Beauty and the Beast is, in Jungian terms, a sacred marriage. This ending portrays a profound transformation brought about through the reconciliation of the internalized captive victim (Beauty) and the internalized degraded abuser (the Beast). The coming together of polar opposites within the Self, a *coniunctio*, is both a sign of and a prelude to the experience of wholeness. It is an expansion of consciousness. Robert Hopcke, a Jungian theorist and psychotherapist, sees the *coniunctio* as "a guiding image and evocative challenge to each individual concerned with inner resolution and outer relatedness."[5] This particular union of opposites is made possible only by the Beast's faithfulness and by Beauty's willingness to love the Beast's ugliness.

The Beast's faithfulness, his love for Beauty even in the face of rejection and abandonment, depicts accurately the faithful quality of denied aspects of the Self. Those parts of the Self that have been rejected as imperfect and beastly—in Jane's language, the Evil Twin aspects—do not disappear, nor do they, once relegated to the unconscious, stop suing for consciousness and acknowledgment, just as the Beast does not accept his relegation to the confines of his enchanted estate. The symptoms produced by these rejected aspects are usually ugly, often involving forms of compulsive behavior that reflect the dominant psychological experience of lack of choice. That ugliness may seem to increase the split between the Redeemer persona and the shadow-Beast. However, it is the ego's perfectionistic clinging to the Redeemer persona that actually maintains that split. The rejected aspects of the Self continue to present themselves —in the mirror, in dreams, in projection onto others, in symptoms of psychological suffering—continually pursuing the possibility of a whole, connected Self.

In the tale Beauty finally responds to this faithfulness with an admission of love in the face of suffering. Deep suffering, to the point of a feeling of psychological and spiritual death, often accompanies the confrontation of the Redeemer persona and shadow-Beast. The pain inherent in a childhood like Jane's, the pain inherent in acknowledging the effect of the victim identification on one's adult life, is immense. An intense, delayed grief response follows closely on increased awareness. Consequently, there is a strong temptation, whenever the pain of confronting the Beast becomes conscious, to avert acknowledgment of the shadow through renewing the quest for perfection (the body is a common target in these quests) or through blaming others and embarking on the endless project of redeeming them.

What enables Beauty to resist those diversions and acknowledge her own connection to the Beast? The dream, the symbolic intervention, provides her with an opportunity to change, but she still must respond with empathy for the Beast, empathy for his suffering, for his faithfulness, for his ugliness itself. This deep empathy requires her to abandon her perfect daughter role, transforming her identity. That transformation leads to love, even for the hideous Beast, and ugliness is then, in turn, transformed by love.

Psychologically this is a moment of empathy for, acknowledgment of, and acceptance of the shadow-Beast. Empathy is enormously misunderstood in the context of relating to the Self and is often confused with the defensive process of rationalizing shadow aspects of the self. Empathy for the shadow, however, is not expressed through making excuses for its actions. It is not a process of blaming others for the presence of an internal Beast, a process epitomized by what Alan Dershowitz, the well known defense lawyer and Harvard law professor, calls the "abuse excuse" in trial defense.[6] Nor is it an attempt to get others to care for the Beast, as exemplified by codependent relationships. Both of these responses prolong victim identification. Ownership, love, and acceptance of the imperfect parts of the Self must happen within a context of responsibility for the entire Self. Rationalizing the negative impact of shadow aspects prevents true internal union and also reveals the fact that the ego does not actually accept the shadow-Beast. The fourth step of the Twelve Steps of AA presents an excellent model: rigorously honest examination of the shadow followed by making amends to those injured by it. When the shadow is accepted, the Redeemer's considerable talent and energy can turn toward her own redemption. This will provide her with a much stronger foundation from which to give to others, should she choose to.

The transformation of the Beast into a prince does not imply that all shadow material can be made pretty. Rather, this is an image that communicates the marvelous relief and transformative magic accompanying real acceptance of the split-off parts of the Self. These aspects no longer seem hideous and unmanageable but become human and manageable. (It is important to note that shadow material is hideous to the individual to whom it belongs but may seem benign or even positive to others.) An incident between Jane and her brother, which occurred late in therapy, illustrates this shift. Jane's brother was in her home and was behaving in a demeaning manner modeled on their father's contemptuous attitude toward women. Previously Jane would have worked very hard (and futilely) to find the perfect way to respond in order to transform her brother's unpleasant behavior into something more workable. This time she simply said, "Perhaps you should go home and return when you are in a better frame of mind." Making this seemingly simple statement required her to abandon her own desire to redeem her brother's loutish behavior and necessitated her accepting her own self-protective aggression—a very shadowy, beastly aspect for her. She felt exhilarated. This example also illustrates a very important distinction: transformation of the Redeemer victim identity requires self-protection from the external Beasts of this world coupled with controlled connection to the internal shadow-Beast. Holding the distinction between inner and outer process is absolutely essential to transformation. Relating to the inner Beast, the shadow, in an accepting, exploratory manner does not sanction bestial behavior toward others, nor does it imply that the bestial behavior of others is acceptable in external circumstances. Internal experience and external behavior are not synonymous.

The final image of the story is powerful and instructive. The sisters are petrified, vividly demonstrating a lack of liminal capacity, forever stuck in place unless and until they develop the ability to reflect upon themselves. This portrays the way in which a life devoid of self-reflection, spent in the quest for gratification from others, leads to a living death, stuckness, a loss of connection and growth. The image of the sisters frozen in stone forcefully illustrates how necessary an internal reflective space is in the process of transformation and how useless blame and projection are, the sisters' usual approach to life and relationships. The fact that Beauty cannot transform her sisters drives home the futility of the project of redeeming others. Viewing the sisters and Beauty as coexistent aspects of the psyche, the ending also makes it clear that even a major transformative experience, like the sacred marriage of Beauty and the Beast, is not the end of individuation. Individuation has no end; some aspects of the psyche are always waiting to be explored, to melt in the light of consciousness and participate in life.

CHAPTER FOUR

VICTIM AS SEEKER

The Youth Who Set Out to Learn What Fear Was

A FATHER had two sons. The elder seemed bright and capable, but the younger seemed good for nothing. One day his father said to him, "All the money I have spent on your education is wasted," and his son replied, "I would gladly learn to shudder." He wanted to know what fear was. His elder brother called him a ninny. His father thought him even more of a fool and went to the sexton to complain of his younger son.

When the sexton heard the whole story, he offered to teach the younger boy to know fear by leaving him in the church bell tower overnight. At midnight the sexton disguised himself as a ghost and crept up to the tower. Not only was the boy not frightened but, he knocked the sexton down the tower stairs.

"Oh," cried his father, "you'll bring me nothing but misfortune! Get out of my sight. Go out into the wide world and do what you will, but tell no one who your father is. I am ashamed of you."

The youth set out on the road muttering to himself, "If only I could shudder." A man heard him and said, "When we come to the gallows at the crossroads, sit down under them and wait till nightfall. You'll soon learn fear." The boy did as the man suggested, and when night fell he built a fire to fend off the cold. After a while he thought the fellows up on the gallows must be cold too so he brought them down to sit by his fire. However, they didn't seem to appreciate it, so he hung them back up. He still did not know how to shudder.

Back on the road he continued to mutter to himself, and this time a carrier overheard him. The carrier took him to a part of the country where there was a haunted castle. It was a terrifying place, full of treasure guarded by evil spirits. The youth went to the king who owned the castle and asked to stay there so that he might learn to shudder. The king wanted his treasure back, and even though no one who went into the castle ever came out, he told the youth to stay there three nights. If he did, the spell on the castle would be broken and the youth could marry the king's daughter, who was very beautiful. The youth could take three things into the castle with him. He asked for a fire, a turning lathe, and a carving bench with the knife attached.

On the first night two huge black cats appeared by the fire. They had fiery eyes and sat on either side of the youth. "Friend, shall we play a little game of cards?" they asked. "Why not," replied the youth, "but first stretch your paws." When they stretched out their paws he screwed their feet to the carving bench and dispatched them. As soon as he did so, black cats and dogs sprang out of every corner, leaping onto his fire and surrounding the boy on every side. Finally he was tired of it all and let fly at them with his carving knife.

The second night he sat by his fire. After a while a terrible din started, and half a man fell down the chimney. "Hi, up there," the youth cried, "there's another half wanted." The din commenced again with shrieking and yelling, and the other half fell down. The halves joined together into a hideous man, who was soon followed by others. They fetched skulls and bones and played ninepins. "Look here," said the youth, "I'd like to join your game, but your balls aren't very round." He took the skulls, put them on the lathe, and made them smooth. "Now the fun begins," he said. He played with them until midnight, when they vanished before his eyes. The next morning the king came, eager for news. "Did you shudder?" he asked. "No such luck," said the boy. "If only I knew what it was."

On the third night six men came in carrying a coffin. "This must be my cousin who just died," said the youth. "Here, cousin, I'll warm you up." He sat the corpse up by the fire. When that had no effect, the boy put the corpse under the bedcovers and snuggled up to it. Finally the corpse warmed up and began to move around. It rose up and said, "Now I will strangle you." The youth picked the corpse up and threw it straight back into the coffin. The six men came and carried the coffin away. "I simply can't shudder," said the boy, "and it's clear I shan't learn here."

Then a giant old man of fearsome appearance

entered. "You will surely learn fear," he said, "for now you must die." "Not if I am the stronger," replied the youth, running down the dark corridors to a forge. The old man lifted an ax and drove an anvil into the ground. "I can do better than that," said the boy. He went over to another anvil, and when the old man bent over to see what he would do, his beard hung down. The boy cleft the anvil with a single blow and jammed the giant's beard in. He then picked up an iron rod and belabored the old man until he whimpered and offered the youth riches. The boy released the giant and followed him down to a cellar where there were chests of gold. At midnight the old man disappeared, and the boy found his way back to the fire and went to sleep.

In the morning the king woke him and asked, "Have you learned to shudder?" The youth said no and told the king all that had happened. "You have broken the spell of the castle. You shall have the gold and marry my daughter. "That's all charming," said the youth, "but I still don't know how to shudder."

After he was married he drove the princess to despair by constantly muttering, "If only I could shudder, if only I could shudder." Late one night she and her maid took a pail full of little fish called gudgeon into the bedchamber and poured them all over her sleeping husband. As they swam and wriggled all over him, he woke and cried, "Oh, how I shudder, dear wife! Now I know what it is to shudder."

Most people find this story strange, even for a fairy tale. The youth seems ridiculous, not just to his father and brother but also to the reader of the story. What does he want from the experience of fear? The youth who set out to learn what fear was is seeking knowledge. He yearns for experience, he wishes to compensate a lack in himself, he wants to be more whole. This victim identity often leads to very strange behavior and experiences, including repetitive involvements with exploitive authority figures—teachers, gurus, political leaders, and so forth. This is an active factor in the development of cults and other similar groups, whose gullible and self-destructive members often seem inexplicable, viewed from the outside, much as the youth in this story seems inexplicable.

The youth seeks knowledge by looking for a guide. When he approaches members of his family for guidance, he is met with contempt and rejection. When he seeks guidance outside the family, he is repeatedly abused. Although the boy escapes relatively unscathed from each encounter, he does not find what he seeks. Those who claim to be able to help him in his quest exploit his trust and use his quest as a pretext to act out their own greed and sadism. This is all too familiar to us. We have read many contemporary stories of Seekers treated in just such a fashion by spiritual or political guides like the Reverend Jim Jones of the infamous People's Temple.[1] The victimized Seeker is also present in private life when an individual idealizes romantic partners as the source of wholeness, seeing that ideal in partners who are exploitive. The victim as Seeker wanders, as the youth does, going from disappointment to disappointment, from failed guide to failed guide, questing for a lost part of the Self. Although the protagonist of this fairy tale is male, as is the main case example used, it is not a victim identity that is exclusive to men.

The Meaning of Seeking Fear

What is the meaning of seeking fear? Of what use is the ability to shudder? In this story the ability to shudder evokes the capacity to have full emotional and somatic response, to be permeable to experience, vulnerable to life. The hero ideal prompts us to see impenetrability and invulnerability as virtues. To be unaffected, calm, and impervious in the face of threat is equated with dignity. Every once in a while a person who is an acknowledged hero figure will admit that fear is natural, saying something like, "Of course I'm afraid, everyone is," and when this happens it is popularly received as a mark of great humanity in the hero figure. However, no one wants to see the hero actually experience fear, that is, to witness him shuddering. That would be shameful.

The ability to shudder requires permeability. The man or woman who shudders is affected by life; he or she allows life to have impact. As the story makes clear, this basic permeability is necessary to survival. Inability to shudder leads the boy into ever more dangerous acts and situations. The boy does not have access to his body's natural responses to danger or to his survival instincts. He has lost his experience of normal human vulnerability, especially the common bodily experience of vulnerability—shuddering. Our culture's commitment to heroism is so extreme that it may be difficult for us to grasp the depth and seriousness of the youth's problem.

The body's vulnerability is especially problematic for the heroic ideal. Plans and fantasies about transcending the body are common in Western literature and philosophy. Christian theology has contributed greatly to this trend by portraying the body as intrinsically sinful, a constant source of downfall. The vulnerable, permeable human body with its natural responses to danger, horror, and threat has become something that must be constantly disciplined, bent to the mind's will, overcome. The body and its wisdom are primary shadow carriers in Western culture. In Victorian times, sexual responses were probably the most demonized aspect of the body's life. Now it may be that vulnerability and need are the most shameful bodily experiences.

The eradication of normal fear is perceived as an essentially masculine virtue. A manly response to victimization, in the culture's popular imagery, is to repress fear and pursue mastery, usually through vengeance. A cursory review of popular film reveals many paragons of contemporary masculine heroism (Clint Eastwood and Sylvester Stallone, for example) who are victimized and respond by mastering their normal horror and fear to the point of numbness. This is required so that they can revenge themselves more efficiently on the victimizer(s). Boys are explicitly taught this response, frequently experiencing ridicule when they show normal fear and upset in response to threat, attack, or unfairness. Although it is not typical for a girl to be directly trained to repress fear, many girls and women share the culture's distaste for normal vulnerability and feel deeply ashamed of their lack of repression. Once again we notice the association of the heroic with masculine gender construction. To show fear is effeminate, contemptible; it makes one a sissy.

Vulnerability, fear, and the spontaneous bodily responses that accompany them are devalued if not rejected outright by the culture and by the typical individual. What, then, is lost to the individual? Returning to the story, we find that, in addition to showing no normal self-protective reactions, the youth seems to feel little joy in life, being obsessed with his quest. Shutting down the experiences of vulnerability dulls the impact of life itself. Becoming impervious is not selective; once the body's spontaneous reactions are shut down, the effect spreads. One is as impervious to joy as to fear. The youth also finds it hard to relate to people, and this too is a consequence of imperviousness. When the youth seeks to shudder, he is seeking to be open to experience, to recover his body's wisdom in the form of its spontaneous responses. He is seeking to be affected by life, by feeling, and by other people.

His lost vulnerability is, in essence, the lost child in the Underworld. The youth has not abandoned that lost child and the potential for true development that it holds. When he laments, "If only I could shudder," he seems to be grieving for his lost openness and seeking an entrance to the Underworld of emotion. The youth reminds us of Demeter in his willingness to stay focused on the recovery of what is lost, even in the face of universal indifference. Unlike Kore, he is without a mother and must act as his own rescuer in this regard, mourning for what is lost and never forgetting it.

Nature and Development of the Seeker Identity

How does normal human vulnerability become shut off in a person? This fairy tale gives us some indications of the roots of this phenomenon in its portrayal of the youth's family and of the local clergy. Father, brother, and sexton all respond to the youth's longing with contempt. No one is concerned with the meaning of his desire to shudder; no one shows any desire to understand him or to empathize with him. All are concerned primarily with the youth's inability to conform to expectation, to perform his role, and to make a proper appearance. The standards of the family are high, rigid, and unconnected to the youth's personality. Deviation from those standards is met with contemptuous words, aggressive actions, and, finally, complete rejection.

Daryl was the oldest son in a family that valued performance and stoicism above all else. As an adult he could succeed at most tasks but he could not form relationships that were not hierarchical. Daryl had employees or mentors but no partners, in business or in personal life. He was often betrayed, both from above and below. Daryl's most striking feature as a client was his pervasive contempt. He felt contempt for women who showed flaws, for men who failed to be heroes, for himself, and, vividly, for his therapist, me. When Daryl was disappointed, as he often was, he responded with contempt for those who disappointed him. When he felt threatened he responded with contempt and aggression toward the threatening person. When he felt longing he responded with contempt for himself.

At the same time, Daryl was a Seeker. He went from mentor to mentor, usually teachers of new age growth techniques, and from betrayal to betrayal. He neither deeply understood nor fully grieved any of his disappointments. All were covered in a blanket of contempt, sometimes for the failed mentor, always for himself. Daryl experienced a complete lack of reflective internal space. He could not reflect on, muse about, or speculate on his most significant experiences. His imagination, emotions, and bodily responses were regularly and automatically dismissed by his internalized contempt, in a type of self-commentary that would remind us vividly of the youth's father in the fairy tale. With no internal reflective space and little access to emotion and imagination, liminality was virtually unknown to Daryl. Dialogue between conscious and unconscious aspects of the Self was ignored.

This contempt was learned at the earliest possible age. Daryl's mother had told him that infants were disgusting and boring. The fact that this was a precise description of Daryl's stance toward his body and emotions made it easy to imagine the force with which his mother's attitude had been conveyed to Daryl in his earliest fundamental relationship with her. Once a child in the family was over the age of four (they were all boys), the mother ignored the child completely, leaving him alone to struggle with his older brothers and father. Daryl's father wanted his sons to glorify the family name through accomplishment. Mistakes were met with extreme ridicule. Visible signs of upset were met with accusations of effeminacy (the worst possible attribute). At the same time, too much achievement would excite the father's envy and he would begin to undermine the achiever through ridiculing his accomplishments. The only safety in this double bind lay in the attempt to be unaffected. And indeed, one of the few traits that father and brothers openly praised in each other was a stoic lack of response. Alice Miller's delineation, in her book *The Drama of the Gifted Child,* of the effects of contempt is helpful in understanding this dynamic.[2] Why does the parent show contempt? "Contempt for those who are smaller and weaker is the best defense against a breakthrough of one's own feelings of helplessness."[3] What is the effect of the contempt on the child? It helps to create and maintain a false self which is split off from "the lost world of feelings."[4]

One of the major losses brought about by Daryl's harsh upbringing was play. Neither Daryl nor any of his siblings played beyond the age of five. The few child-like games the brothers played were essentially exercises in ruthless competition, games of dominance. Free play, which normally allows children to express their inner world, was unknown and extremely dangerous in Daryl's family. This free play, which requires a safe atmosphere, is the developmental foundation for the liminal capacity we discovered in the figure of Persephone. In healthy development the safe container provided by the atmosphere of a family that allows children to be children can be internalized by the child. The transformative speculation, the liminality of play itself, is safe to pursue. This lays the foundation for an ego that can build such containers in adulthood, can perceive and value a safe emotional atmosphere in future relationships. The internalization of this foundation allows the ego to participate in symbolic dialogue, which is a playful activity, and to take a stance that is open to the spontaneous communications of the Self. Daryl was closed to those communications, and he could find no safe relationships.

As an adult Daryl slowly became aware that he was missing something. However, he had no idea what was missing. Unlike the youth in the tale, Daryl had no conscious memory of maternal feeling for his lost openness. As is often the case with those who have ingested and identified with contempt (a form of identification with the aggressor), he was only conscious of his longing and his loneliness. He was aware of his isolation but unaware of its fundamental cause —his own impermeability, his own lack of vulnerability. The contempt he felt for the spontaneous responses of his body and emotions, the ridicule he had been taught to heap on the liminal state that is key to inner transformation, cut him off from the internal gateways to change and left him caught in constant seeking. His ego consciousness had identified completely with the aggressor, and as a consequence even his seeking was done in contemptuous ways. He felt eternally disappointed and victimized while others experienced his contemptuousness as abuse.

Over fifteen years of clinical practice I have found that the Seekers I have treated have shared many characteristics with Daryl, and their histories have shared many factors with Daryl's history. All had little or no sense of real childhood. They were expected to know more and do more than is usual for children. True child-like behavior was worthless and even dangerous. Requests for help or understanding were inconceivable. An explicit family ideology glorified the suppression of most normal responses, especially responses of vulnerability and self-protection, and demonized all forms of ambiguity or ambivalence. The families of these clients conflated love with conformity, and deviations from the family's ideology were met with rejection and abandonment. The children were subjected to constant scrutiny of both deed and thought.

These conditions are internalized and live on in the adult as an embedded, habitual disconnection in the way ego relates to Self. The developing ego has difficulty in acknowledging and validating normal vulnerability and shows a tendency towards perfectionism. The perfectionism is incorporated in consciousness as a set of abstract, disembodied rules for all situations. These rules act as a particularly thick and constraining filter, screening out from the Self all emotional, somatic, and symbolic communications that might deter the ego from identifying with the family's rigid value system. Spontaneous responses are deeply distrusted. The intensity of this identification, necessary for survival in families where personal choices are severely punished, begins to blot out the normal, self-protective "no" response to overly intrusive authority figures, a "no" that usually rises up in a spontaneous reaction of the kind most likely to be suppressed by the family ethos. Instead, an overly rigid "no" response to liminal, playful, or ambiguous experiences becomes almost automatic, effectively cutting off the Self's line of communication to the ego.

The ego tends to hold self-sufficiency as the highest value, and the true Self is experienced as intrinsically burdensome to oneself and to others. Talents and abilities are not experienced as real or enjoyable unless they fit the rules. Aspects of experience that do not fit the rules are met with blame and dismissal. Blame is experienced as natural, whether it is aimed inward or outward, and is valued over compassion. Blame becomes conflated with morality and ethics. The Seeker moves through life in an atmosphere of harsh judgment and even harsher demands.

Adult Seekers: Idealization and Disappointment

It may seem confusing to say that Daryl's seeking was done in contemptuous ways since he idealized his series of mentors, at least for a limited time. However, his idealization of a mentor always included contempt for others. He elevated each new mentor by comparison with contemptible past guides, and he felt elevated by his scornful view of his fellow followers. Some Seekers still feel contempt for themselves when they idealize another, but their relationship to the ideal other allows them to imagine that they will be transformed. Idealization forms a small refuge from contempt, a refuge containing only the Seeker and his mentor. It was the only refuge Daryl ever had from his relentless scorn, and it disappeared when disappointment with the mentor, which is the inevitable consequence of extreme idealization, set in. The cyclical process of idealization and disappointment is a key aspect of the Seeker victim identity, an unconscious way of trying to work out the legacy of contempt.

Cathy Rose, in a phenomenological study of idealization and disappointment, has explicated some key dimensions in this cyclical process, and her findings are congruent with my own clinical experience.[5] The chronic idealizer has a fundamental feeling of loss, an orphaned feeling, and hopes the idealized figure will act as "a gatekeeper who provides entrance into a special place . . . a home . . . where one's being can shine forth in a special way."[6] Being raised as Daryl was disconnects the ego from the internal resources that can provide each person with a sense of unique and valuable selfhood. Contempt had taught him to scorn internal guidance, so he thought that he must find a transcendental other to guide him to the place where he could be free of scorn. We have touched on this special place before in our discussion of the container.

The Seeker is driven by an accurate sense of what he or she needs—a strong relationship with someone who will perceive the Seeker's unique qualities and help the Seeker gain access to his or her own resources. The Seeker seeks a person or group who will provide the container that will allow the Seeker to be open to life and feelings again—to shudder. Such a relationship could provide the container, the special place required to transform the orphaned feeling. So why don't the Seeker's relationships work? Why does the Seeker go from failed relationship to failed relationship, disappointment to disappointment? As we see in the story of the youth, being raised with scorn impairs the ability to form accurate assessments of others. The youth trusts the wrong people. So did Daryl. The Seeker's formative experience with scorn predisposes him to two potential distortions in assessing and relating to people, especially people who might be of help to the Seeker.

The first distortion springs from the adult Seeker's ongoing identification (sometimes conscious, sometimes not) with the family's ideology. Virtue, safety, and love are closely associated with demands for conformity, productivity, perfectionism, and the suppression of self-protective impulses. Charismatic leaders or ideological communities that use scorn and contempt to "teach" their followers are particularly difficult for Seekers to see accurately. The family's ethos of stoic invulnerability invalidates the spontaneous emotional and somatic responses that warn of an unwholesome, exploitive situation. The Seeker does not acknowledge the hints of emotional danger that spring from the gut level when one is in emotional peril. Like the youth sitting under the gallows, the Seeker's inability to shudder cuts off the awareness of danger at its roots. Consequently, Seekers are susceptible to people and movements that re-create their families' oppressive ethos, and these relationships reinforce the original wounds. Continued identification with the family's ideology may also cause the Seeker to be abusively contemptuous and exploitive to others, without the perspective necessary to realize the damage.

The second distortion in Seekers' ability to assess relationships is somewhat more complex and is an aspect of their attitude toward others. Although Seekers are prone to choose mentors and guides who re-create the oppressive atmosphere of their families, they occasionally connect with people who are not exploitive or harsh. Despite this, the relationship often ends in disappointment. The contempt that Seekers feel for themselves and others is communicated in a variety of verbal and nonverbal ways. In any intimate relationship the atmosphere of judgment and pressure produced by this self-righteous scorn can call up a parallel response even in people who are normally kind and accepting. This is a psychological process known as projective identification. One feels the internalized contempt of the Seeker as if it were one's own; it bubbles to the surface either as scorn for oneself or as scorn for the Seeker. Few people have a way of conceptualizing or dealing with this process. Consequently, normally kind and accepting people may find themselves withdrawing from the Seeker or, alternatively, being harsh to him. Both are unconscious efforts to protect one's vulnerability from the barren inner world of judgment that rules the Seeker's inner life. Both reactions leave the Seeker abandoned again, this time because the internalized world of judgment and contempt has contaminated a potentially healthy situation.

The Seeker moves from person to person, sometimes from group to group, organization to organization, experiencing longer and shorter cycles of idealization and disappointment in his quest for a way back to himself. Frequently sexual and romantic relationships are infused with the idealization-disappointment process. The Seeker is effectively boxed in—tending to be drawn to people who are contemptuous and tending to treat others in a way that brings scorn and rejection into all relationships. Just as the youth who is seeking to learn fear suffers repetitive disappointments when he asks those he meets for help, the Seeker seems to find it difficult to learn from his disappointments so that they will not be repeated.

Cathy Rose delineates several stages in what she calls the "aftermath of disappointment," the process a person goes through when an idealized figure lets him or her down.[7] One stage includes the process of reflecting on the question, "Who am I in my own right, apart from the idealized figure?" Responses to this question lead to new capacities and insights, which help to prevent a repetition of the disappointment. The individual who identifies with the Seeker victim persona does not go through these stages in processing disappointment. Instead, he tries to handle disappointment by finding a new figure or organization to idealize. The Seeker is haunted by the loss of the idealized figure and longs for a new idealized relationship, despite the obvious damage done by the one that has failed.

Attachment to the Seeker Identity

Attachment to the Seeker victim identity is motivated primarily by an intense fear of accepting the personal shadow. For the Seeker, accepting the shadow means consciously experiencing vulnerability, dependency, grief, and rage. Although this could be said of almost anyone who needs to deal with the shadow, the effort is particularly demanding for Seekers. The attitude of contempt that dominates all attempts at observation, introspection, and analysis in the Seeker makes it especially difficult for the ego to be matter-of-fact about shadow material. The Seeker's ego is so identified with the heroic, stoic ideology of the family that it is prone to a fantasy defense of imagining that the shadow material can be made to disappear. In many ways it is this magical service of eliminating the shadow that the Seeker's ego hopes to receive from his idealized guides. Consciously, the Seeker wants those he idealizes to provide a relationship and tools for removing the normal human shadow. Unconsciously, the repressed aspect of the Self, which is the child lost in the Underworld, is seeking the relationship that will allow the shadow and the other split-off parts of the Self to emerge. It is that emergence and acceptance that bring an end to the orphaned feeling.

The constant search is compelling, then, both in terms of keeping the shadow at bay and in terms of reconnecting to the Self. However, the family ethos has inculcated the Seeker's ego with the sense that the true Self is not an ordinary human experience but an extraordinary experience available only to a favored, hard-driving few. Contempt for normal vulnerability and need makes it almost impossible for the Seeker's ego to contemplate access to the transcendent Self through the shadow, the repository of such imperfect human qualities as fear, rage, or vulnerability and the home of extremely difficult family memories. The ongoing drama of idealization and disappointment that accompanies the quest serves to keep hope alive while providing a constant distraction from internal life, where the shadow predominates. Holding to the quest preserves the fantasy of great specialness.

The Seeker has an extreme reluctance to give up on what is owed to him. This is an advantage in one way; it is analogous, as has already been noted, to Demeter's loyalty to her abducted child. It is an important remnant in the ego of maternal concern for the tender Self, which was cut off and distorted by contempt. However, since this sense of being owed something is usually pursued in the absence of accurate self-knowledge, it fuels the unfulfillable quest for release from the shadow. In other words, the conscious image of what is needed is formed by the victim identity. The ego's identification with the family ethos (which often coexists with despising individual family members) makes it difficult for the Seeker to come to an accurate sense of what is actually owed to him—that is, a safe place to experience liminality and reconnection to the Self, the paradoxically ordinary and extraordinary potential he shares with all humanity. Instead, the healthy drive for wholeness is attached to an image of perfection and grandiose specialness.

The Seeker finds it difficult to accept and process the grief and disappointment that followed the losses that have already occurred. Instead, habitual judgmentalness colors the sense of having been cheated of something. This tends to manifest as a blaming attitude toward others rather than as compassion for the losses of the Self. A turning point must be reached in the ego's attitude before compassion is possible.

The Seeker's Turning Point

What are the conditions and experiences that interrupt the cycle and provide an opportunity for the Seeker to truly complete his quest? The youth's experiences on the road are repetitive. They yield nothing for his quest, and they all resemble, in emotional tone and in structure, his initial disappointments at home. This reflects the cyclical experience we have just discussed. Although the youth has left home—indeed he cannot even acknowledge his home or name—his experience tells us that he has not separated from the role he had at home. He re-creates on the road his old family identity of fall guy; the first aspect of a rite of passage has not been achieved. As in *Beauty and the Beast,* this separation from the family role identity, which allows him to move into the transformative liminal stage of initiation, takes place within the walls of an enchanted castle.

Unlike the youth's encounters with darkness in the church tower or on the road, his experience in the haunted castle is focused and committed. He makes a commitment to the king which means he cannot move on as soon as he is disappointed. This is a key to the resolution of the Seeker's quest. In everyday life such a commitment may take various forms. The Seeker may commit to a person that he or she knows, objectively, is not exploitive or hurtful. It takes both insight and an act of will to give up the more grandiose, idealized relationships and to commit simultaneously to processing the difficulties that inevitably emerge in a more real relationship. Or the Seeker may commit to coming to a true understanding of his quest as well as of the internal world and personal history from which the quest springs. The first type of commitment allows a container to develop within a relationship. The second type allows a container to develop within the Self, an internal reflective space. Both types of commitment prevent the Seeker from pursuing his usual solution to disappointment—looking for the next ideal. Instead of fleeing at the first taste of descent and disappointment, the youth must stay on and experience the descent in full. This is what the Seeker needs to do.

The king to whom the youth commits himself is an interesting figure who undergoes a shift in the course of the youth's experience in the castle. At first he seems to be like the other people the youth has encountered—exploitive, greedy, and unconcerned with the boy's quest. But over the three days of the youth's descent into the darkness of the enchanted castle the king develops an interest in the youth and in what the youth is seeking. I think this represents both the type of person with whom the Seeker needs to form relationships and the type of ego the Seeker needs to develop.

The king soon evinces a simple, direct interest in the youth's desire to know fear and in his desire to reconnect to his body's spontaneous responses. And, unlike anyone else the youth has known, the king actually admires the youth's competency. The Seeker needs relationships with people who take a straightforward interest in him, who try to perceive his strengths and weaknesses clearly. The Seeker may need to have this kind of relationship first with a therapist in order to know what it feels like.

The Seeker must then develop an analogous interest in himself, an ego stance that allows exploration unburdened by judgment and contempt. He must begin to consider the support and tools he needs and then find them. He needs a stance that allows him to interact with the things that rise up from inside himself without immediately moving on to the next panacea. In other words, he needs to consider the answer that spontaneously arises from within rather than continue searching for a grander, ideal answer. The Seeker needs psychological tools for detaching from his old identity, for confronting the shadow material that at first dominates inner life.

And here, too, the Seeker is better equipped to meet the darker aspects of life when he enters the haunted castle. He requests tools—a fire, a turning lathe, and a carving bench with the knife attached. The fire brings the light of consciousness to the contents of the unconscious. The carving bench symbolizes the ability to fix chaotic and potentially overwhelming complexes while exploring them. The turning lathe conveys the capacity for interacting with and making use of unconscious material. The knife supplies a keen edge of analysis and aggression in dealing with pathology. The Seeker is now more prepared to enter into the container that will lead to the culmination of his quest.

The Haunted Castle

In the castle the youth finally engages in the first stage of initiation, separation from his family role as hapless incompetent. His sojourn in the castle is a descent into an Underworld, the second stage of initiation. His experiences are the experiences we have when we confront the unconscious. The youth first confronts menacing cats and demonic animals, then dismembered people who play with human bones; he has another close encounter with a corpse and, finally, a contest with an enormous old man. These encounters give us some indication of the nature of the Seeker's necessary confrontation with the unconscious. Once the Seeker is able to make a commitment to exploring and examining his experience, approaching the Self with an interested rather than contemptuous attitude, he becomes conscious of the shadow in its various forms. This description of the youth's sojourn in the castle gives us a sense of the nature of Underworld transformation.

The fiendish cats and attacking animals convey the intensity of the Seeker's suppressed rage. It is both the rage that results from being ridiculed as a child and the outrage that springs from the loss of access to the true Self. These feelings are intense and invasive once they are no longer contained and expressed through contempt. The Seeker must experience these feelings without dumping them on other people. The rage must be connected back to the people and situations that engendered it, and the outrage must be used to fuel the development of the Self. The fundamental work of acknowledging the effects of personal history and working through the legacy of childhood wounds is essential to dealing with the shadow.

On the second night in the castle the youth meets dismembered men. When the ego's attitude has caused many aspects of the Self to be ignored, the unconscious becomes the refuge of many undeveloped parts. These men are gruesome in aspect, as many undeveloped parts of the Self appear to be, but, interestingly, they have come to play a game. On this second night the youth is not actually in danger as he is on the first and third nights. Instead, he must find a way to play. He interacts without having to kill or destroy. He mediates his interaction with these aspects of the unconscious by changing the forms of the skulls; he is meeting them but not solely on their terms. This seems to be a playful, liminal episode, symbolizing a psyche in which the tool-bearing ego begins to use those tools in order to interact with the unconscious.

During the youth's last night in the castle he has another encounter with a corpse, echoing his experience under the gallows. How is death involved in the Seeker's quest? The hero persona is, in many ways, a fantasy protection against death. The ultimate sign of impermeability is indifference to death. The youth is unaffected by corpses, and his standard response to them seems to be to try to revive them. He doesn't seem to grasp death as real, and this may be because he is not completely open to life. A part of him is deadened already. He cannot grieve a loss because he does not really take it in; he is still impermeable. On another level the youth's constant efforts to revive corpses are connected to his quest to awaken his own deadened body.

The youth's final adventure brings him face-to-face with a giant old man who has a scornful attitude. This old giant symbolizes the way in which the family's ideology of scorn for vulnerability looms large in the inner life of the Seeker. It must be actively fought and invalidated. The internalized scornful voice of the family's contempt for vulnerability and uniqueness must be stopped in its tracks. Cultivating an awareness of the inner scornful voice holds it in place, just as the old man is held in place by his beard. The recovering Seeker must be willing to actively belabor this ingrained attitude—to confront, challenge, and ultimately repudiate it. This process is straightforward but requires awareness. It is only when the youth has dealt with this scornful and competitive, overpowering male that he can lift the malign enchantment and enter into a new kind of relationship, this time with a woman. He enters the third phase of a rite of passage and has a new identity, radically different from the identity available to him in his family.

Recovering Spontaneous Responsiveness

The youth's quest is fulfilled through the actions of his wife and her maid. He learns to shudder, not through his heroic actions or by following the advice of a mentor, but through a new kind of relationship. The recovery of the body's responsiveness and openness to experience must take place within the container of a trusting relationship. The princess and her maid portray a down-to-earth approach to the youth's quest and they choose a direct approach to the recovery of the body's responsiveness. His wife is frustrated by his obsession, as everyone is, but unlike everyone else she chooses a body-oriented way of helping him. This is a most helpful kind of relationship for the Seeker. The common-sensical, ordinary quality of the women's intervention is a very important counterbalance to the inflated, unrealistic expectations with which the Seeker has typically been raised. A person who is straightforward, simple in the sense of not being grandiose, and who has no vested interest in exploiting the Seeker can provide him with a pivotal experience, especially if that person has a direct and unambivalent relationship to the body. But the youth's marriage tells us more than that; it depicts a reunion between two parts of the Self, the seeking ego and the responsive Self.

Why is that part of the Self portrayed as a woman? Women as individuals and the feminine as an archetypal force are perceived as having a special connection to vulnerability and a special access to the body's wisdom. As we have discussed in connection with the myth of Persephone, the victim's initiating descent frequently involves coming to terms with aspects of the Self seen in our culture as feminine. Our cultural attachment to the masculinized hero stance tends to valorize a hyper-rational, somewhat grandiose but at the same time alienated approach to experience. This approach dominates the Seeker's conscious attitude toward self and life. "Could it be that the body is the unconscious and that in repressing and, more important, disregarding the spontaneous life of the nervous system we are enthroning the rational, the orderly, the manageable?"[8] It could be just that. It is not surprising that the playful "mother wit" needed to resolve the Seeker's quest is brought to him by a female figure, the feminine being associated with the shadow of the rational and orderly. The princess embodies the connectedness, the openness to experience that the Seeker has been seeking; she is the functional opposite of his invulnerable persona. The princess and her maid provide a liminal, mediating connection between the youth and his body's spontaneous responses, his experience of playfulness. The youth's new wife finds a way for the youth to experience his body as subject, not object. Let me emphasize that the gender imagery here is symbolic. Seekers are not necessarily male. However, the Seeker victim identity has an association to the masculine gender role and the Seeker needs to gain access to feminine aspects of the Self for balance and renewal. This is another form of sacred marriage.

The coming together of polar opposites within the Self, a *coniunctio,* is both a sign of and prelude to the experience of wholeness and an expansion of consciousness. Through his relationship to his wife and her maid, the youth brings these opposites together within his own body and recovers his fundamental responsiveness. He shudders. This reconnection gives the Seeker a ground for continued individuation. The ego that is grounded in relationship to the body has a foundation and a container for dialogue with the Self and with nature. Someone like Daryl must develop interest in and respect for the spontaneous offerings of the Self that form the basis of symbolic dialogue; he must recover some appreciation for what he has previously scorned—human play. These spontaneous experiences may seem trivial to an ego that has been taught to hold inflated and superhuman standards. The little fish that teach the youth to shudder are an excellent image for the usual forms of symbolic dialogue, the everyday guise of the unconscious. As I have said before, "the experience of inexplicable revulsions and allurements, gripping moods and body states that appear to have little or no basis in external events, compulsive behaviors, seemingly random thought streams, intense responses to people—any or all such experiences may spring from the unconscious."

It is difficult for a Seeker to give up his attachment to the heroic, large-scale quest, the quest that promises to make him more than human, in order to cathect these seemingly small communications from within. But, ultimately, the search for an experience of the transpersonal must go through the mundane. The Seeker must value being simply human before a wholesome connection to the transcendent potential of the Self can be effected: Those who recover the body's responsiveness may experience what Charlene Spretnak calls "grace," an oceanic, bodily experience in which the interrelatedness of all things can be felt rather than merely speculated upon.[9] This type of experience has been pathologized by mainstream values, which glorify perfect autonomy and separateness as the ideal of psychological health. It may be this experience that the Seeker seeks in spiritual communities.

Separating the value of spiritual practice from the pathology of exploitive leaders and communities depends upon acknowledging the past experiences of exploitation in detail. Internalized distortions in the image of and relationship to the Self are brought out, acknowledged, and processed when these experiences are explored as specific incidents, not generic experiences. The Seeker needs to focus on: (1) the way in which he conflates love with agreement or conformity, and (2) building internal tolerance for ambiguity and seemingly oppositional truths. In the context of a therapeutic relationship, it is extremely important that the therapist form an alliance with the Seeker that allows exploration of these issues without imposing a new system—

the therapist's worldview—on the Seeker. The Seeker's desperate need for guidance often evokes a countertransference impulse to give advice, promulgate new rules, and give a template for living.

Psychotherapy with the Seeker

The Seeker generally approaches psychotherapy in one of two modes. He may still be "seeking;" in other words, the therapist may be approached as the next subject for idealization. Alternatively, the Seeker may come into therapy as a "last resort," in a state of cynical exhaustion and determined to have minimal expectations for the experience. This is a brittle protection from the cycle of idealization and disappointment. When a therapist is approached by a Seeker in the first mode it is extremely important that the therapist resist the pull of idealization. To be told that one is the answer to someone's prayers is tempting to most people. The therapist must be interested in exploring the idealization without being drawn into it. When stories come out in the course of the therapy about previous authority figures and helpers who became disappointments, it is important to connect those previous relationships with the current one. The Seeker's ego's protestations ("I'm sure you would never be like that") aside, it is reassuring to the Seeker's Self to have a relationship in which idealization is not the basis of the connection and in which the other does not need unreasonable admiration. When the idealization begins to fade the negative transference will emerge.

When therapy is approached in the second mode, of cynical, low expectations, the negative transference is apparent at the beginning. In this instance the therapist has the burden of carrying hope for the process and the difficulty of working with a client who is careful to avoid real connection with the therapist. The negative transference, composed of extreme mistrust alternating with withdrawal, must be tolerated and compassionately understood both in terms of the adult history of seeking guidance and being exploited or at least disappointed, and in terms of the family history. Simple but straightforward reflections of the mistrust and withdrawal must be made as they are expressed, directly and indirectly. Slowly the connections can be made between the feelings brought alive in the therapeutic relationship and the exploitations, disappointments, and betrayals of the past. Empathy is often greeted with intense hostility, both as an affront to the contempt-laden demands of the Seeker persona and as a temptation to trust again, with all of the attendant possibility of disappointment.

Daryl came into therapy with a mixture of these two presentations, and this is not particularly uncommon. His intense desire to idealize me was under a cover of cynical contempt about therapy—much of the contempt expressed in silly terms, since Daryl was rather uninformed about therapy. I made the very important mistake of not taking this cynical defense seriously enough. I paid no attention to the subtly contemptuous and hostile remarks he made about me and about therapy, and instead I began working immediately with Daryl's history of idealization and disappointment, reaching back into childhood. In this misjudgment I also may have been falling into the temptation of expressing indirect contempt, in the form of dismissal, for his cynical defense, reacting to protect myself from the atmosphere of scorn that suffused Daryl's approach to himself and to others. At first this mistake was not very noticeable. Daryl found enormous relief in being able to tell the stories of his disappointments and having them compassionately understood. His relationships outside therapy improved, for a time. Therapy began to balance some of the distortions in his ego's view of his shadow. The shadow was the needy child abandoned by his mother at age four. But by bypassing the negative transference, by ignoring his thinly veiled hostility, I had neglected to make room in the therapeutic container for Daryl's considerable rage. The more he became aware of the fundamental betrayal of that child aspect of the Self, the more angry he felt.

My task was to help him disentangle wholesome anger from the hostile bitterness that took its form from his father's nasty scornfulness. Daryl needed to embrace the anger that reflected a wholesome concern for his exiled shadow child. This first type of anger, which in the terms of this discussion would be analogous to Demeter's wrath, could provide Daryl with the impetus for bringing that shadow material into consciousness, for bringing the child back from the Underworld. This was rage in the service of individuation. In Daryl's psyche, it was mixed together with a bitter contempt, the legacy of childhood victimization, a recursive defense that could produce a new victim persona rather than real change. Unfortunately, Daryl and I were unable to maintain our balance in this task, for several reasons.

First, because I had not been attentive to the negative transference when it came up at the beginning of treatment, we had little practice in working together directly on Daryl's anger. We had primarily worked on his anger at others, outside the therapy and in the past. Rarely had Daryl been very angry when actually sitting in the room with me. Consequently, we began trying to find a way of processing his anger under the pressure of intense feelings and with little practice. Second, Daryl's contempt for women, which was an amalgam of his necessary, inevitable fury at his mother's abandonment of him and of his father's contempt for anyone perceived as vulnerable, became highly aggravated. As long as this contempt was aimed at me it presented an opportunity for us to bring its component parts to consciousness. However, Daryl began to act these feelings out in a series of romantic relationships marked by intense, mutual emotional abuse.

Daryl was, as far as I could tell, treated very badly by the women with whom he became involved. At the same time his intentions toward these women were openly sadistic. This repetitive acting out of the contemptuous side of his rage and his wish that I would support its sadistic components made the healthy aspect of his anger extremely difficult to delineate and support. Finally, Daryl retreated from this impasse in therapy by finding a new guru, who was very happy to be idealized and to collude in Daryl's disdain for women.

Why have I chosen to use an example of failure in therapy? I have worked with Seekers for whom the slow process of recovering the spontaneous responses of the emotions and the body was successful. Why not use one of these successful examples? First, I feel that it is important for therapists to occasionally report failure, to honestly present the very real, inevitable potential for failure in the process of psychotherapy. This is important both for prospective clients, who frequently come into therapy with idealized images of the process (especially if they are Seekers) and for other therapists, who certainly know that they fail occasionally but who rarely see that experience dealt with in psychological literature. Second, the processes of idealization and disappointment are so powerful in the Seeker's psychotherapy that the story of a failure may be as instructive as the story of a success.

What does a successful completion of therapy look like for a Seeker? Lynn, another Seeker, was able to address the contempt she sometimes felt for herself and for others. After coming to a better understanding of my experience with Daryl, I was more alert to the negative transference, and through processing it, Lynn and I came to terms with her hostility. As a consequence we began to build, within the therapeutic relationship, a container that provided the reflective space necessary to reconnect to the resources of the Self. Over time Lynn began to recover her liminal capacity, to be able to value dreams, fantasies, bodily sensations, and emotions, to reflect on them and consider their meaning. Some years after the end of the work I did with Daryl I heard from him again. After going through another terrible disappointment with his new guru he went back to therapy, this time with a male therapist, and he had begun to recover his responsiveness to life.

The Seeker's Connection to Spiritual Life

"In fear we tremble. We shiver and shake as we encounter the dreaded unknown. . . . Fear is the primal affective source of sacred imagination and the compensatory ideal of the holy."[10]

Seekers form a desire for spiritual sustenance early in life. They respond to deprivation by seeking connection to the *anima mundi,* the world soul. Why some children do this while others do not is not clear to me; it may have to do with some person they are influenced by, or it may be a function of temperament. Their connection to spiritual life is skewed by unresolved shadow material. Once the Seeker has disidentified from the victim persona and contempt is no longer the dominant attitude toward the Self, the shadow can, as a consequence, be addressed. If the victim persona and the shadow are being consciously worked through, they will no longer skew the Seeker's spiritual quest. Then the Seeker's capacity for and interest in spiritual life can be pursued, as long as there is an adequate, wholesome container for it.

Ritual practice provides a container and a felt experience. As the Seeker recovers spontaneous responsiveness it is important that his or her spiritual practice be more than an abstract set of concepts. In a spiritual practice that includes ritual, the Seeker may experience what anthropologists call *participation mystique,* which is the phenomenon of experiencing a personal identification, a "oneness" with the transpersonal.[11] The transpersonal may be embodied in a group, in nature, or in spiritual experience.[12] In *participation mystique,* subject and object are united. The experience is felt rather than speculated about. A living, potent ritual is a visceral experience, not an acted-out metaphor or an expression of social convention. "In ritual, knowledge is neither just described nor explained; it is embodied and sensually experienced."[13]

A variety of communities have sprung up that pursue

different kinds of ritual practice. Assessing the efficacy of a particular community's rituals, in terms of container or depth of experience, may be almost impossible to do from outside the practice. Goddess groups are, for example, highly visible communities that have renewed ritual practice. Such groups tend to be small and extremely diverse in quality. It is vital that the Seeker, with his or her proclivity for idealizing authority figures, choose a spiritual community that is clearly nonexploitive and well organized in its power structure. A clear and fair power structure gives the Seeker a safe container in which to pursue spiritual life.

The youth who set out to learn what fear was undertook a quest for recovered responsiveness. The Seeker is on a quest for relationships that will help him transform fear into awe, contempt into self-acceptance. Once free of shadow distortions, his spiritual orientation can become part of a deeper response to life.

CHAPTER FIVE

VICTIM AS PARIAH

Manypelts

ONCE upon a time a king had a wife so beautiful that her equal was not to be found on earth. It came to pass that she became ill and called the king and said, "If you wish to marry again after my death, take no one who is not quite as beautiful as I am; this you must promise me." And after the king had promised her this, she closed her eyes and died.

For a long time the king could not be comforted and had no thought of taking another wife. At length his councilors said, "This cannot go on. The king must marry again, that we may have a queen." And now messengers were sent about far and wide to seek a bride who equaled the late queen in beauty. In the whole world, however, none was to be found. Now the king had a daughter, who was just as beautiful as her dead mother and had the same golden hair. When she was grown up the king looked at her one day and saw that in every respect she was like his late wife, and suddenly he felt a violent love for her. Then he spoke to his councilors: "I will marry my daughter, for she is the counterpart of my late wife." When the councilors heard that, they were shocked, and said, "No good can come from such a crime, and the kingdom will be involved in the ruin."

The daughter was still more shocked but hoped to turn him from his design. Then she said to him, "Before I fulfill your wish, I must have three dresses, one as golden as the sun, one as silvery as the moon, and one as bright as the stars; besides this, I wish for a mantle of a thousand different kinds of fur and pelts joined together, and one of every kind of animal in your kingdom must give a piece of his skin for it." For she thought, "To get that will be quite impossible, and thus I shall divert my father from his wicked intentions." The king, however, did not give up. When all was ready, the king caused the mantle to be brought, spread it out before her, and said, "The wedding shall be tomorrow."

The king's daughter saw that there was no longer any hope of turning her father's heart, so she resolved to run away. When everyone was asleep, she got up and took three different things from her treasure: a golden ring, a golden spinning wheel, and a golden reel. The three dresses of the sun, moon, and stars she placed into a nutshell, then she put on her mantle of all kinds of fur, and blackened her face and hands with soot. Then she walked the whole night until she reached a great forest. And as she was tired, she climbed into a hollow tree and fell asleep.

She was still sleeping when it was full day. The king to whom this forest belonged was hunting in it. His huntsmen said, "A wondrous beast is lying in the hollow tree; we have never before seen one like it. Its skin is fur of a thousand different kinds, but it is lying asleep." Said the king, "See if you can catch it alive." When the huntsmen laid hold of the maiden, she awoke full of terror and cried to them, "I am a poor child, deserted by father and mother; have pity on me, and take me with you." Then they said, "Manypelts, you will be useful in the kitchen. Come with us, and you can sweep up the ashes." So they put her in the carriage and took her home to the royal palace. There they pointed out to her a closet under the stairs where no daylight entered, and said, "Hairy animal, there you can live and sleep." She lived there in great wretchedness for a long time.

It happened, however, that one day a feast was held in the palace, and Manypelts got the cook's permission to go upstairs and look on. She went into her den, put off her dress of fur, and washed the soot off her face and hands, so that her full beauty once more came to light. And she opened the nut and took out her dress that shone like the sun, and when she had done that she went up to the festival. The king came to meet her, gave his hand to her and danced with her, and thought in his heart: "My eyes have never yet seen anyone so beautiful!" When the dance was over she curtsied, and when the king looked round again she had vanished, and none knew whither.

She had run into her little den, however, and there quickly taken off her dress, made her face and hands black again, put on the mantle of fur, and again was Manypelts. And now the cook said, "Make me the soup for the king; I, too, will go upstairs awhile." Manypelts made the best bread soup she could, and when it was ready she fetched her golden ring from her little den and put it in the bowl in which the soup was served. When the dancing was over, the king had his soup brought and ate it, and he liked it so much that it seemed to him he had never tasted better. But when he came to the bottom of the bowl, he saw a golden ring lying there, and could not conceive how it could have got there. Then he ordered the cook to appear before him.

When the cook came before the king, the king asked who had made the soup. The cook replied, "I must acknowledge that I did not make it; it was made by the hairy animal." The king said, "Go and bid it come up here."

When Manypelts came, the king asked, "Who are you?" "I am a poor girl who no longer has any father or mother." He asked further, "Of what use are you in my palace?" She answered, "I am good for nothing but to have boots thrown at my head." He continued, "Where did you get the ring that was in the soup?" She answered, "I know nothing about the ring." So the king could learn nothing and had to send her away again.

After a while, there was another festival, and then, as before, Manypelts ran into her den, washed herself quickly, took out of the nut the dress that was as silvery as the moon, and put it on. Then she went up and was like a princess, and the king stepped forward to meet her, and rejoiced to see her once more, and as the dance was just beginning they danced it together. But when it was ended, she again disappeared so quickly that the king could not observe where she went. She, however, sprang into her den, once more made herself into a hairy animal, and went into the kitchen to prepare the bread soup. When the cook had gone upstairs, she fetched the little golden spinning wheel and put it in the bowl so that the soup covered it. Then it was taken to the king, who ate it and liked it as much as before. Manypelts again came before the king, but she answered that she was good for nothing else but to have boots thrown at her head and that she knew nothing at all about the little golden spinning wheel.

When, for the third time, the king held a festival, all happened just as it had before. And now she put on the dress that shone like the stars and thus entered the hall. Again the king danced with the beautiful maiden and thought that she never yet had been so beautiful. And while she was dancing, he contrived, without her noticing it, to slip a golden ring on her finger, and he had given orders that the dance should last a very long time. When it was ended, he wanted to hold her fast by her hands, but she tore herself loose and sprang away so quickly through the crowd that she vanished from his sight. She ran as fast as she could into her den beneath the stairs, but as she had been too long and had stayed more than half an hour she could not take off her pretty dress but only threw over it her mantle of fur, and in her haste she did not make herself quite black, but one finger remained white. Then Manypelts ran into the kitchen and cooked the bread soup for the king, and as the cook was away, she put her golden reel into it. When the king found the reel at the bottom of the soup, he caused Manypelts to be summoned, and then he espied the white finger and saw the ring that he had put on it during the dance. Then he grasped her by the hand and held her fast, and when she wanted to release herself and run away, her mantle of fur opened a little, and the star-dress shone forth. The king clutched the mantle and tore it off. Then her golden hair shone forth, and she stood there in full splendor and could no longer hide herself. And when she had washed the soot and ashes from her face, she was more beautiful than anyone who had ever been seen on earth. But the king said, "You are my dear bride, and we will never more part from each other." Thereupon the marriage was solemnized, and they lived happily until their death.

In the story of Manypelts a beautiful princess escapes from a dangerous and degenerate home by making herself into a disgusting pariah. The environment of her home and her relationship to her father and his court make it impossible for the most beautiful and expressive part of her, her true Self, to remain in plain sight. This part of the princess becomes a fugitive, concealed behind the persona of a victimized outcast, a disgusting semi-bestial creature. The Pariah persona progresses from being a necessary survival strategy to becoming a way of life. Even after the princess escapes her father, she continues to live as Manypelts in the new kingdom. Finally, the princess's true Self is released from this victim identity when she is truly recognized.

Psychologically, the experience of being a Pariah may be projected onto one aspect of the self, frequently the body, or it may subsume the entire sense of self. This leprous sense of self can be carefully hidden behind an extremely perfectionistic facade or, conversely, cultivated as an almost aggressive outward repulsiveness. Eating disorders and depression are frequent aspects of this persona. Just as the princess in the story has a number of hidden virtues and secret strengths that must be recognized and developed, the individual caught in this victim identity has internal resources that are not obvious. The process of revealing the buried virtues of the Self is a powerful part of this story.

Origin and Development of the Pariah Identity

The Pariah victim identity is an extreme and debilitating persona, and it typically develops in extreme environments. The clients I have known who struggled with this victim identity came from homes rather like the one described in the opening paragraphs of Manypelt's story—families in which a parent is intent on exploiting a child in some grossly inappropriate and damaging way, just as the king is intent on using his daughter to incestuously relieve his loneliness, regardless of the damage done to her. These are families in which no one is able or willing to intervene and stop the abuse, just as the king's courtiers are unable to stop actions that they know are wrong. Intrusiveness and possessiveness and frequently incest are common in these families. In such hopeless and overwhelmingly unwholesome environments, a child begins to suppress and hide the most appealing, special, and precious parts of the Self, both in an effort to stop attracting destructive attention and in an effort to preserve the Self, to keep it safe from exploitive adults. The mask hiding the Self is the Pariah persona, a victim identity that simultaneously incorporates the unwholesome atmosphere of the home and makes the child less appealing to current and future exploiters.

Mike was referred to me by a local HMO group. The assessment made of him by the psychiatric department of the group was confused. They did not seem to know if they were referring him because he was not disturbed enough to warrant prepaid treatment, even if he wanted it, or if they were referring him because he was too disturbed to be successfully treated with the short-term therapy approach they used. When Mike called to make his first appointment, he seemed personable and intelligent. As the day of his appointment approached, however, I felt more and more uneasy. I began to be afraid to meet with Mike at a time in the early evening, when the office suite would be otherwise empty, even though I knew nothing about him that would cause this fear. Since a fear of this kind is extremely unusual for me, I took it seriously as a possible intuition. The materials I received from the HMO included a release of information from Mike, that is, permission to discuss his treatment with appropriate care providers, so I called the intake worker there who had interviewed Mike and referred him to me. She said that Mike had been perfectly appropriate with her but that the way he looked at her gave her "the creeps."

I was unsure of what to make of my and her covert perceptions, but this odd division in perception continued as I got to know Mike. My conscious perceptions of him were that he was a fairly ordinary man who had never developed his intellectual or artistic potential and who suffered from a mild but persistent self-doubt. My unconscious perception of him, expressed in stray thoughts and images, somatic sensations, and dreams, was that he was in the grip of repulsive and dangerous obsessions. After consulting with a therapist whom I considered to be very adept in listening to the unconscious, I decided to mention my sub-rosa apprehensions to Mike, albeit in a very toned down form.

In response, his secret life came pouring out, an intense, inchoate mixture of sadistic and masochistic fantasies. I began to fear that I had made a serious mistake and that I would not be able to contain and process this flood of obsessive imagery, much of it about me and other authority figures. Finally, drawing on Alice Miller's straightforward understanding of the way in which childhood abuse is recreated in adult life,[1] I said, "I wonder what happened to you that made you feel that it is exciting to be hurt and exploited by people who are supposed to care for you."

This brought the fantasies to an immediate halt. Mike appeared confused and looked very young. Haltingly, over the next months, he began to reveal the secret life of his family. Mike's mother used him as a surrogate husband and companion. Although she never actually had sex with Mike, she undressed him and undressed in front of him until he was a teenager. She confided in him about her sadomasochistic sex life with his father. His father was also sadistic in his behavior toward the children, beating them and terrorizing them without interference from the mother or anyone else. Outwardly the family presented an extremely bland, devoutly religious facade. Mike had completely identified with this configuration, his bland facade covering a frightening brew of uncontained exploitive and destructive impulses that were the legacy of his upbringing. He believed these hidden impulses to be the sum of his true self.

The spark of the Divine Child, the potential of the unique Self, was deep in the Underworld. Mike's parents were both abductors of the Kore part of himself, and there was no one in his world to mourn or search for the lost spark, to play the part of Demeter. Whenever Mike's parents caught a glimpse of the magical, special quality of the child's Self, they pounced on it and used it for their own purposes—his mother to increase her exclusive, eroticized hold on his emotions, his father to act out his sadistic and envious feelings. Mike internalized these responses, and they formed the basis of his ego's response to any messages from the unconscious. Every time an inspiration or insight, some communication from the buried Self, came up into Mike's conscious awareness, he either used it as the basis of a violent erotic fantasy or held it in abusive contempt. He had taken on the Manypelts identity, clothing himself in the bestial clothing of a Pariah in order to survive his parents. However, he had not yet found the new castle that Manypelts found, the place that would enable the true Self to come back into consciousness without being exploited. Mike's Self had been dragged into the Underworld at a very young age, and the only sign that any part of him was working for a return—the only visible fragment of a Demeter-like aspect to his consciousness—was his somewhat confused desire to be in therapy. The unique potential and transpersonal power of his Divine Child aspect was squirreled away, like the magical dresses Manypelts hid in the nutshell.

Hiding in the Forest

When the princess transforms herself into Manypelts and runs to hide in the forest, she is performing an act of desperation that has two aspects: one reflects hiding and giving up, the other reflects seeking. First, she submerges the true Self behind a bestial mask to save herself from her exploitive, ruthless father and to hide from a world that has betrayed her. The child who has the experiences that Mike had, who is forced to identify with a Pariah persona in order to survive, tends to have a profoundly cynical view of human society. Manypelt's experience gives her no reason to believe that people will respond to her helpfully or appropriately, nor did Mike's experiences. People around them were variously blind, impotent, or complicit in abuse and exploitation. So Manypelts escapes to the forest, a form of the Underworld where the Self can become lost, showing only the bestial, Pariah persona to the occasional passerby.

Most often this Pariah identity is vested in a body image. From a symbolic perspective, the body in Western culture is a container for everything irrational, tainted, dangerous, chaotic, engulfing, and out of control. This meaning-image of the body is deeply internalized by many people in Western cultures. In my own psychotherapy practice I have noted that self-hatred can live fundamentally and intractably in the body. This basic reality contributes in an obvious way to the eating disorders and exercise disorders that are endemic among those with a Pariah persona. Demonization of the body contributes less obviously, but perhaps seminally, to a wide range of debilitating distortions of identity and self-image that people suffer, a range that might be summed up as forms of self-loathing. Many forms of self-loathing originate in bodily experiences like physical child abuse and incest. Even when the roots of distorted self-image lie elsewhere, in experiences that are not physical abuse, the body may easily become the repository of the feeling experience of self-hatred. As a consequence, people often feel that the body must be molded, disciplined, and scrutinized but also, paradoxically, ignored as a source of joy or wisdom.

When we read of Manypelts taking on her animalistic persona, covering her natural beauty with a nonhuman facade and cowering in the woods or underneath the stairs, these profound word images resonate with an internalized sense of the body as essentially vile. The feeling of being beautiful is lost for the child when adults respond to that beauty with exploitation, envy, dismissal, or aggression. The body, the young child's primary carrier of identity, begins to carry a feeling of taintedness, a feeling that is vividly supported by cultural associations of the body with sinfulness. Mike viewed his body solely as a means to an end. He went on many unusual diets, involving various kinds of deprivations but showing little physical benefit. He exercised with devotion, taking particular pride in exercising despite painful injuries. When Mike was ill he felt chiefly impatience and disgust with his body. In his image of and relationship to his body, Mike directly expressed his internalization of and identification with his parents' attitude toward his body and his entire self: he was there to be used no matter what the effect on him of being used. In adulthood Mike perceived his body, his feelings, his talents, and his sensibilities as things to be used—by himself and by others. His sadomasochistic fantasies depended on this attitude.

Hiding in the forest is a retreat from such exploitation and is also a retreat to nature. The Self takes refuge in a part of life that is removed from human society and that may provide some nourishment when human society has failed. From this point of view the forest embodies a mysterious resource that is not entirely human, that is transpersonal. For some people who are being victimized in intolerable, inescapable ways, the forest symbolizes a literal and deep relationship to nature; the natural world provides both solace and a sense that there is more to life than human treachery. For others the forest lies in their dreams and fantasy life. For still others art or religion becomes a refuge that also provides meaning and a form of emotional nourishment. The animal-hide cloak, which is the princess's outcast persona, reflects the two-edged nature of her retreat to the animal world of the woods. It is an echo of the cloak made of small animal pelts (especially cats) worn by Teutonic witches in very old stories, favored by them for its association to Freya, the Nordic Goddess of Life. This aspect of the Goddess is very ancient, reflecting the Mistress of the Animals manifestation, one of the earliest images of the sacred feminine. It is interesting that this archetypal image survives in this Teutonic folktale, hinting at the paradoxical quality of Manypelts's retreat to the forest. She is both hiding and seeking, seeking a connection to the transformative, archetypal resources of the unconscious symbolized in the image of the cloak and the hollow tree. For the tree also may be a remnant of a very old image, Yggdrasil, the Tree of Life. The Self has been driven deep into its primordial layer, connecting to ancient images of nature and nourishment, in an effort to find a resolution to Manypelts's terrible situation. This transpersonal lifeline sustains her until she encounters a new king and is consequently introduced to a new household, a court and castle very different from her father's. The new king embodies the ego attitude required to bring the Self up from the Underworld of degradation and self-loathing. It is necessary to reconnect the transpersonal resources that have been relied upon for survival to the everyday world of human society. This is analogous to the stage of Demeter's journey in which she brings her archetypal mourning into the world of a family.

Mike had both artistic and psychic talents, which served him as transpersonal resources. His innate talent for drawing was a source of pleasure to him and was helpful in his work. Mike was also likely to experience synchronistic events; he frequently dreamed of an event that would happen soon after the dream, and he would find that many times images from his thoughts and conversations would appear in his environment. During one therapy session we spoke of his fondness for roses and he walked out of the office building to find a dozen roses on the sidewalk. Mike retreated into these realms frequently in childhood and adulthood, and his experience of them reflected the paradoxical nature of the retreat to the transpersonal level of experience. His artwork tended to repetitively reflect, and to a certain extent vent, the pressure of his sadomasochistic fantasies, and so it sometimes seemed to be a part of the Pariah persona. At the same time, his art would occasionally reveal a jewel-like potential and burst of life.

Mike's occasional clairvoyance and predilection for synchronistic events was sometimes incorporated into his victim identity by making him feel extremely odd, not fit to be a normal part of society and deserving of persecution. "In the old days they would have burned you at the stake," his father frequently said. At the same time, these very meaningful experiences kept alive a feeling of numinous connection to the world in the face of degrading childhood circumstances. Mike's ego attitude needed to move from his parents' model of cynical, ruthless exploitation of the Self to respectful interest in and appreciation of his talents, gifts, virtues, and flaws. Mike needed to develop a stance toward himself that would allow him to recognize the resources and strengths of the Self hidden in his unconscious, an approach that would allow those resources to develop in ways not dictated by his experience with his parents.

Recognizing Hidden Aspects of the Self

The hidden treasures, which the princess who becomes Manypelts takes with her when she escapes her father, are symbols of the survival of the transformative power of the Self, even in the most adverse circumstances. Some of these treasures appear as unique, precious intrusions into the ordinary stew of life, showing up as hints, like the little golden wheel at the bottom of the king's soup. Other hidden treasures, like the sun, moon, and stars dresses, give a more complete image of the hiding Self, in that the dresses imply a hidden aspect of identity. The Pariah persona is, once again, so extreme and so limited as a way of life that the individual caught in it may well have a extremely different and well-developed internal identity, whether he is aware of this or not. I am not speaking here of multiple personality disorders, in which "alternate" personalities live through different aspects of one person's life, but rather of a hidden and undeveloped Self that has not lived much at all.

At first the hints of the Self that are embedded in everyday life are crucial. Recognizing and following up on these hints paves the way for the emergence of the hidden aspects of the Self. This process is the beginning of symbolic dialogue between the ego and the unconscious. In "Manypelts" it is the king who catches the hints; his character demonstrates the growth of a new ego attitude, one that is required for symbolic dialogue. When he sees Manypelts in the forest he is interested in her as a "wondrous beast" and cautions his huntsmen not to injure her.

After this it seems that he forgets her and she lives under the stairs, in the ashes of the kitchen "in great wretchedness." This tendency of the ego to step forward and take an interest in a "wondrous beast" found in the forest of the unconscious and then to forget about it, regressing to a persona identification, is a common event. However, the Self, acting through the unconscious, soon throws out more hints. The king is tested, as is the ego in these situations. He responds to the beautiful, mysterious princess who shows up at his ball. Well, who wouldn't? But when he follows up on the golden ring in his soup and is confronted with Manypelts in her full shadow aspect, he does not follow through. There is a back-and-forth development between ego and unconscious in which the hidden Self is revealed in all of its specialness, as when the princess dresses in her magical gowns; then the unconscious returns to the shadow problem, as when the king is confronted with Manypelts in her repulsive aspect. The small golden treasures hidden in the food that Manypelts cooks link these two aspects. Although the king notices these less-obvious signs of the hidden Self and tries to grasp the meaning of these hints, he cannot fully understand the dual nature of the Manypelts/princess. This back-and-forth process parallels the development of a new ego attitude; the ego is slowly building up the capacity for symbolic dialogue, developing an approach to the Self, through the unconscious, that is accepting and exploratory rather than exploitive.

In Mike's psychotherapy this back-and-forth process took place through dream work. Mike had a rich dream life, which he typically interpreted in a distorted fashion, reflecting his parents' view of him. For example, if Mike dreamed of an evil figure, he thought it was a symbol of himself. If he dreamed of a positive figure, it was never an aspect of himself. In effect, he was habitually clothing the Self in a cloak of pelts. When he told me these dreams I reflected his habitual approach back to him, linking it up to its source in his personal history. I also offered a few thoughts and responses to the dreams that came from a different, more respectful stance, while being careful not to be overbearing. Slowly this modeling affected Mike's attitude toward the symbolic communications of the unconscious.

Why is this one-step-forward-two-steps-back process necessary? Mike is an adult now, no longer controlled by his parents. What keeps him in thrall to the persona that suited them? Once Manypelts is away from her dangerous father, why doesn't she fling off her hairy disguise and stand openly revealed in her beauty?

Attachment to the Pariah Identity

The reasons for a continuing attachment to the Pariah persona are two-edged: some reasons are regressive, tending to increase the victim's entrapment, and some are progressive, tending to further individuation. The regressive aspects of attachment to this victim identity have a lot to do with the extreme specialness that can be associated with the kind of exploitation Mike suffered as a child. There is "a feeling of omnipotence . . . a sense of being the sin-carrier . . . and thus one chosen and unusually strong."[2] This self-image springs from being expected to carry a role that is far beyond the normal capacities of a child. The intensity of Mike's mother's incestuous attachment to him, her willingness to act on it, and her demands that he respond, distorted his individuation and deformed his relationship to the Self. It also inflated him, making him very special, chosen over his father, big enough to carry the family's sickness.

He had what Jungian analyst Sylvia Perera, in her study of the scapegoat complex, calls a "curious pride and pleasure"[3] in this role. As an adult, Mike often found, or was found by, people who were happy to have him perform this same role for them. The perverse power of his position often blinded him to its self-destructive consequences. He was deeply disappointed that I was unwilling to have an affair with him or, failing that, unwilling to allow him to give me gifts or do work for me, such as painting my office. My refusal to exploit him made him feel small and weak. When people accepted his direct and indirect, verbal and nonverbal offers to be used, he felt excited, strong, and purposeful.

While his Pariah persona carried his family's collective shadow, Mike's personal shadow, the key to the individuation of his unique Self, was the small, dependent child who needed protection in order to begin to reconnect to the Self's true path of development. Free play was impossible in an environment where any sign of creativity, inspiration, or spontaneous affection would either bring overwhelming, smothering attention or a sadistic beating. No container or reflective space could be internalized or maintained by the ego as a safe place for symbolic dialogue with the unconscious to develop. The Pariah persona is a protective cloak for this small, needy shadow who is waiting for a safe place, for a container formed of nonexploitive relationships in which to find its own path of development. Attachment to this protective covering is progressive in that individuation would not be served by abandoning that protection unless the environment were truly safe, and so a certain amount of waiting and unconscious testing is necessary, as we see in this fairy tale and as emerged in Mike's psychotherapy.

Detachment from the old, family-based identity, the first stage of initiation, is particularly difficult for the Pariah, and because of this his considerable liminal capacity (the second stage of initiation) cannot be used in the service of individuation unless and until a new kind of containing relationship is developed.

The New Container

Manypelts puts the king through three tests in which she makes a delicious soup with a golden surprise in it—a ring, a tiny spinning wheel, and then a golden reel. Although the king is interested in these hints of Manypelts's true nature, he fails to fathom their meaning the first two times. When he questions her directly about what and who she is, she is sullen and rather bitter: "I am only good to have boots thrown at my head." This reluctance to reveal the hidden Self when asked manifests in the Pariah identity both interpersonally and intrapsychically. Mike, and other psychotherapy clients I have worked with who had a similar history, tended to withhold information in interpersonal relationships as a matter of course. Other people had proved to be so untrustworthy that he behaved as if anyone might gain an advantage over him with any piece of knowledge he revealed. Mike was also upholding the family's virtuous facade by withholding information about his past. Others, and especially authority figures, had to be tested repeatedly to make sure that they were really interested in the Self, that they really wanted to know the truth, that they were not intent on exploiting the Self, and, most important, that they were capable of perceiving the value of the Self, even when that value was not obvious.

Intrapsychically a parallel pattern evolves between the ego and the unconscious. The ego, which is identified with and dominated by the Pariah persona, receives hints and clues from the Self through the medium of symbolic communication from the unconscious. These peeks at the Self are often tantalizing, like the delicious soup Manypelts makes and the little treasures she places in the bowl. In Mike's case these hints came in beautiful, transcendent dreams and in the synchronistic events he experienced. But following up these clues brought Mike face-to-face with disturbing material, just as the king, standing here for the ego, is brought face-to-face with Manypelts in her most inhuman, unappealing aspect. The ego must turn a corner here and be willing to try to recognize the potential within the devalued parts of the Self, must be willing to accept and work with the shadow in order to have access to the transformative potential of the Self.

The shadow that usually accompanies the Pariah persona is an unusual one. Having incorporated, identified with, and carried the family's shadow as an outward identity, the ego has to repress many positive qualities, which become a positive shadow. The phenomenon of the positive shadow is curious and confusing. The talents and straightforward virtues of the Pariah are carefully hidden and covered with a patina of shame. When they are noticed by others they are usually denied or even pathologized by the Pariah himself. Whenever anyone took notice of Mike's artistic talent, he immediately told them that he only liked to draw sadomasochistic subjects, even though this wasn't actually true. He would then describe such an image. Most people were repulsed by this. The few who responded well often had less than good intentions toward Mike. Thus Mike's attitude toward and characterization of one of his most positive attributes tended to push away people with good intentions and to attract those with worrisome intentions.

This type of behavior is an aspect of the Pariah's outer perversity. It is directly modeled on the family's characterization of Mike as a naturally perverse person, a characterization necessary to his role as the carrier of the family's shadow. That role was challenged whenever Mike was perceived by anyone outside the family as a talented or appealing little boy. When Mike as a child showed a special talent or positive trait his mother would praise him, with that praise almost always leading to an eroticized encounter of some kind. Thus she appropriated Mike's positive qualities into her shadow activities. When Mike was recognized by those outside the family, for instance by a teacher, his father would attack him verbally and sometimes physically.

The aspect of the shadow that is congruent with the cultural concept of negative traits is weakness and neediness. Mike's shadow included a very young and desperately needy aspect of which he was very ashamed, and it included also many positive aspects, such as intuition, sensitivity to the needs of others, artistic vision, and self-assertion. This somewhat curious mixture meant that when Mike's hidden talents were recognized and/or rewarded he would feel endangered. This was because recognition of a positive aspect of shadow activated his awareness of the other, weak and needy shadow aspects and also because of the fact that the positive shadow traits endangered Mike's identification with the Pariah persona. The slow revelation, in therapy, of Mike's positive shadow traits and the accompanying emergence of his childlike feeling of smallness were interrupted by many retreats into his Pariah identity, just as Manypelts retreats to her den below the stairs.

Mike's evolving view of himself was accompanied by a necessary reevaluation of his personal history. This was difficult for several reasons: first, it challenged his fundamental loyalty to the family, especially to his mother; second, it aroused his rage; and third, it confronted him with a philosophical problem concerning the existence of evil. Within the family, loyalty was defined as a willingness on the part of the children to see the parents as they wished to be seen. Mike's mother in particular wished her son to see her as a magical, life-enhancing force. As he began to disidentify from the Pariah persona Mike saw the destructive and intensely narcissistic dimensions of her mothering. That meant that Mike could no longer perform this positive mirroring service for his mother.

As he was willing to see the hidden Self more clearly and to acknowledge the historical circumstances that forced it into hiding, Mike began to feel rage for the first time since he was two years old. This was the rage of Demeter, the rising up within the Self of a protective maternal rage bent on defending the precious potential of the Divine Child. Mike's ego was disidentifying with the aggressor. His Hades-like ruthlessness toward his own resources and Zeus-like ignoring of the damage done to him as a child began to shift, and he struggled to develop a normal, interested, and nurturing stance toward the orphaned aspects of the Self. This process was complicated for Mike because of the fact that his only historical model for expressing rage was his sadistic and out-of-control father. How was Mike going to distinguish between wholesome rage and destructive sadism?

The shift in internal attitude that made it possible for Mike to gain access to the Self hidden behind the mask of the Pariah identity brought him face-to-face with both his personal shadow and his family's shadow. Previously he had carried the collective family shadow without having a conscious relationship to it. He also became unavoidably aware of his personal shadow, in part a very dependent, helpless, and abandoned child. Disentangling these interwoven strands of highly charged memories, feelings, and needs was a tricky, long-term process requiring a sturdy container of relationship.

Relationships

Finding the safe relationship, the interpersonal situation in which one can be seen without being treated ruthlessly, is crucial to developing a new intrapsychic balance. The new ego stance must be internalized from a new type of relationship. When Manypelts leaves her family she enters a new environment, a new castle-container as it were, in which she experiences both regressive and progressive relationships. With the cook she has a regressive relationship that is a blatant, outwardly exaggerated, but inwardly trivial version of her exploitive family relationships. The cook's dismissive, demeaning remarks together with his willingness to use Manypelts as a virtual slave reflect the essential nature of Manypelts's father's attitude toward her. In this re-creation of the earlier relationship, disregard and exploitation are not dressed up in any pretty trappings or rationalizations as they were at her father's court. At the same time, the cook is not meaningful or powerful in Manypelts's inner world as her father, the incestuous king, was. The relationship with the cook supports but did not create the Pariah persona.

Victims with a Pariah persona usually have at least one and often several relationships that are obviously abusive and exploitive. While the Pariah identity is in place it can appear that the individual "deserves" this treatment because of his or her perverse behavior. The fact that Mike habitually hid his best qualities combined with the way his obsessive sexual concerns tended to distract him from career goals meant that he never focused on work effectively or got anywhere in his career. Consequently he remained in low-status jobs of the kind that are livable when one has a considerate boss and absolute hell when the boss is insensitive. Interestingly, Mike always had a boss who was, at the very least, insensitive, and often his bosses were outright abusive. In addition, Mike frequently felt that his bosses were respectful of other employees but demeaning toward him. How can we understand such a history? Bad luck doesn't really account for such a consistent pattern. Did Mike unconsciously choose abusive bosses? Is projective identification at work here, infusing a neutral situation with aggressive tension springing from the unconscious pressure carried by the Pariah?

It is important to understand these adult re-creations of abusive family relationships without either blaming the victim or encouraging a codependent type of exaggerated personal responsibility. When Mike's boss was abusive to him, her behavior was fundamentally her ethical responsibility. Mike was not in charge of her behavior. At the same time

Mike often seemed to go out of his way to bring out the worst in authority figures, and he never tried to protect himself when he was attacked or exploited. The Pariah persona is extremely provocative, and even fairly sensitive people may find themselves tempted to act like the cook in the fairy tale. People with sadistic impulses will justify their abusive behavior by citing the Pariah's provocations. When the king shows an interest in Manypelts, he is met with a sullen and provocative response. To his credit, he does not respond abusively but neither does he persist in his interest when rebuffed. As a result, Manypelts goes through a cycle of ascents and descents, coming above the stairs as both Pariah and princess, going back below the stairs when her tests are not met. Below the stairs she does nothing to protect herself from the cook's bad behavior.

These dynamics mean that it can be very difficult for the Pariah-identified person to find the relationship necessary for developing an effective container, a container that will allow the hidden aspects of the Self to emerge and develop. Friends, co-workers, and partners who are tested in this repetitive fashion often lose patience, withdrawing from intimacy and for excellent reason. Typically only people with either sadistic or masochistic tendencies will stay in relationship with the Pariah throughout these unending cycles. Those with sadistic impulses will act them out on the Pariah, who will not defend himself or herself. Partners with masochistic impulses will allow the testing, the repeated disappointments of presenting and withdrawing the Self, to go on indefinitely without resolution, giving the masochist ample opportunity to suffer and blame himself or herself. Neither response is helpful or satisfying to the

Pariah, although he or she may appear to be "asking for it," that is, behaving in ways that encourage and support both sadism and masochism in the partner.

For these reasons the Pariah generally finds the relationship he or she needs in psychotherapy. A well-trained and self-aware therapist will not respond to the sullen, perverse provocations, will not withdraw from the relationship in response to the periodic withdrawals of the Self, and will not allow the cycle of testing to go on without being addressed. Of course she will feel the pull to do one or more of these things as the therapeutic alliance deepens and she begins to experience the conscious and unconscious pressure that surrounds the Pariah (the intake worker's "creeps" and my indirect fears early in the therapy were communications of this unconscious pressure). While all of those who identify with victim personae can benefit greatly from psychotherapy, I do not believe that all victim identities require psychotherapy for transformation. However, the Pariah identity has such a profoundly distorting effect on all interpersonal relationships and on the intrapsychic connection between ego and Self that psychotherapy may be the only reliable intervention for this victim persona.

It is important that the therapist be willing to work slowly and carefully in the process of helping the ego separate from the Pariah persona. Once the family history begins to come out and the therapist realizes the source of the Pariah's perverse and provocative behavior, it is tempting to become a rescuer. In an effort to relieve the scapegoated child of the burden of the family's collective shadow, the therapist might be tempted to say, in effect, "You aren't all bad, they are all bad." This approach is problematic for a number of reasons. It perpetuates and supports the splitting dynamic that produces a Pariah identity. The therapist is talking as though it's healthy to have a Pariah to carry the collective shadow as long as you choose the right person in the family to do it; in effect, "you aren't the real Pariah, your mother is." This approach ignores the part of the ego that is attached to and gets something from the victim identity. The identity is both a burden and a mark of specialness.

The therapist needs to hold one aspect of Demeter's stance, that of advocating for the Divine Child lost in the Underworld and never forgetting the hints given of the potential Self, and she must find ways of empathizing with this Self. However, this must be done without supporting the Pariah persona, which is a legacy of the family's abuse and dangerous to both the victim and his or her associates in life. The therapist must be very aware about what part of the Self she empathizes with and supports. The demands and pressures that are generated by the persona will make the therapist feel tainted, often physically. She must depend on gut-level responses much of the time in order to distinguish between the Pariah's aspects of Self. Of course, this requires the therapist to know herself fairly well so that she can accurately track these responses. She must also be able to contain and process any sadistic or masochistic tendencies within herself.

As Mike's therapist, I often felt conflicted about his expressions of self-hatred. On the one hand, they could be cries of pain and exile coming up from the repressed, child-like aspect of the Self lost in the Underworld of the unconscious. On the other hand, Mike's mother often used self-deprecating remarks as a way of drawing Mike into sympathy with her in a prelude to an inappropriate, eroticized intimacy. The Pariah identity had adopted this ploy, identifying with the mother's shadow and carrying it as part of his service to the family's shadow, using self-deprecating remarks to draw people into an inappropriate merger with Mike. Intellectually I could not sort the problem out any further, but I found that my stomach knew the difference between the language of the persona and the language of the lost child. I learned that if I responded compassionately to expressions of self-hatred that made my stomach tense up while I listened to them, then Mike's Pariah identification would increase, in the form of intensified sexual acting out (unsafe sex with strangers). If I responded compassionately to expressions of self-hatred that felt straightforward and engendered no somatic tension, more of the positive shadow-child would emerge in therapy. I realize that this sounds less than precise, and it is difficult to find language that does justice to the epistemology of the gut. In fact, my body and my basic emotions were better at assessing the wholesomeness of the source of these kinds of communications than my intellect was. I suspect this is often the case and that the therapist needs to take a cue from the Seeker's tale and listen very carefully to the body's spontaneous responses for guidance in treating the Pariah.

For the Pariah, psychotherapy is an attempt to develop and internalize a new ego attitude, embodied in the fairy tale by the new king, a stance toward the Self that is no longer modeled on the parents' exploitive and distorted view of the child. The therapist tries to model this new stance while reflecting on the source, purposes, and effects of the old attitude toward the Self. The therapist tries to embody and call upon some of Demeter's loyalty to the Divine Child, who is unseen but still alive in the Underworld of the unconscious.

The therapist also needs to call on her own mediating ability. She must maintain a balance in which she attends to the somewhat taunting hints and clues of the hidden and undeveloped Self, empathizing with the positive shadow aspects and with the very young, needy shadow elements without inadvertently colluding with the parental introjects (parts of the client that carry the internalized parental values). This requires a therapist who is herself fairly comfortable in the Underworld, who takes the darker side of human nature seriously but is not overly intimidated by it, who like Hecate is able to watch over the client while he or she resides in the Underworld.

The therapist will need to accept and mediate rage as it emerges, playing the Rhea part in striking a livable bargain about the past. Mike's rage was frequently directed at his wife and at me. He often expressed his anger by demeaning both of us as a way of compensating for his previous extremes of loyalty to his mother and, by extension, all women, and also because he had internalized his father's sadistic mode of anger. Acknowledging the legitimacy of Mike's anger while not colluding with the Pariah-based sadism required constant attention, with guiding perceptions often springing from my somatic experience and from Mike's dreams.

Dreams are often an important aspect of therapy's mediating function. Mike's dreams were powerful and dramatic in their imagery. I learned, over time, to take considerable guidance from his dreams. At crucial points in therapy, his unconscious would comment symbolically on the therapeutic process. A turning point occurred in the therapy when Mike dreamed of driving a watertight car into a lake and settling to the bottom with the headlights on so that from within the air bubble contained in the car he could observe the lake bottom. On the same night I dreamed of going to the shore and watching a car, with its headlights on, drive into a lake. This synchronous dream event gave us the imagery we needed to build an alliance around dream work. It also made it clear that, in the collective unconscious, our work was already proceeding and needed conscious acknowledging. Mike's ego consciousness needed to descend into the unconscious within the safe confines of a closed container and with a careful observer on shore. When the safety of good boundaries and helpful self-observation were incorporated into Mike's ego, he was able to experience descent and transformation more directly.

It is crucial that the Pariah find and maintain non-exploitive relationships that will help him internalize a reflective inner space, a psychological container. Psychotherapy with a therapist who is cognizant of the issues described above is the most direct way to address this process. Other important relationships can also provide the mirroring and recognition necessary for transforming the Pariah identity.

Mirroring, Recognition, and Transformation

I have focused on the testing, provocative nature of Manypelts's cycle of revealing and withdrawing the Self, the game of throwing out hints but refusing to answer direct questions. Although this strategy was made necessary by the trauma she had endured and the danger she had experienced at home, her strategy has other, more progressive aspects. As I mentioned before, the coat of many pelts harks back to the ceremonial garb of the goddess Freya and her priestesses, who came to be called witches. Manypelts's magical dresses representing the moon, sun, and stars, dresses that can somehow fit into a nutshell, also indicate the way in which her retreat from her father's court takes her deep into the archetypal resources of the unconscious. The dresses are also aspects of the Goddess in her cosmic form. So when Manypelts alternates between her identities of hairy animal and princess garbed in cosmic dress, she is oscillating between the Mistress of Animals aspect and the Queen of Heaven aspect of the old Teutonic Goddess. As she runs up and down stairs doffing and donning different disguises, dropping and denying hints, she evokes a spirit of play and farce.

Manypelts has liminal capacity in the sense that she is a shape-shifter, and this is generally true of the Pariah-identified victim. People that I have treated who identify with the Pariah persona generally have a playful, medial aspect, reflected in artistic interest and ability, in psychic phenomena, and in the tendency to manipulate their appearance, frequently through the medium of an eating or exercise disorder. Unfortunately, this liminality retains little or no hint of personal freedom and enjoyment. The liminal capacity itself has been enlisted in the service of the family's need for a scapegoat. The transformative potential inherent in liminality, the potential for developing a truer, more individual and personal identity, has been short-circuited by the absence of a wholesome container. Melodramatic as it may sound, the liminal capacity and its power to transform have been co-opted for evil, decadent purposes, much as Hitler co-opted the transpersonal power of ancient Nordic myth for evil purposes.

To rectify this perversion of individuation, two types of recognition must occur. Just as the king, when he notices the white finger, recognizes Manypelts while she is still in her hairy animal form, the Pariah must have relationships with people who recognize the positive shadow aspects while the Pariah persona is in place. Recognizing the positive shadow and the innocent needy child within occurs in a series of moments rather than in a single dramatic revelation. These moments of recognizing the hidden aspects of the Self build to a manifestation of the Pariah's other self, the transpersonal aspect clothed in cosmic garb. The second type of recognition needed is of the transpersonal aspect of the Self. These aspects of the Self, personal and transpersonal, must also be brought into relationship with each other.

Because the Pariah has used transpersonal, archetypal energies to carry his or her family role, the Pariah needs a transpersonal container in order to recognize that role. If this is not available, the power of the archetypes activated in the Pariah may subvert new ego attitudes. In my experience either a spiritual practice or the practice of an art form is necessary for expressing and containing these transpersonal energies. Such practices are also helpful in the necessary task of coming to conscious terms with the evil the Pariah has experienced. For Mike, art became a way to form a philosophical relationship with the existence of evil.

When the Pariah develops relationships with people,

both a therapist and others, who are capable of recognizing and willing to mirror any aspect of the Self that emerges, the Pariah will begin to individuate in ways that go beyond the victim identity. Reflection and feedback from others who are interested but not narcissistic in their interest is crucial to the transformation of the Pariah persona.

Shadow Carriers

Although I have used a white male as an example of the Pariah victim identity, it is important to note that this persona is more prevalent among those who belong to social groups seen as "other" by the dominant culture. A cultural level of shadow projection on an outcast group intensifies the Pariah victim identity and makes it more intractable. As a woman I see this most clearly as it applies to women.

Returning to Perera's discussion of the scapegoat, she states,

> . . . being needed because one is inferior or hateful or loathsome is deeply felt by many women. . . . Women have generally carried, along with minority groups, the collective shadow of heroic Western consciousness. . . . Glorified by themselves and the collective (society) as chosen ones, and equally despised as illicit, alien, second class and victim, they are too often the silent and patient vessels of necessary but derogated shadow qualities.[4]

If a woman has a personal history that fosters a Pariah persona, she will find much in her culture's imagery of women to support that identification and she will find little that provides a refuge from it. Perera assumes that the shadow-carrying dynamic applies to all disenfranchised groups, and this makes sense to me also. I am not able to describe how the culture's shadow is carried by groups whose experience is far different from my own, but it seems reasonable to assume that people who identify with the Pariah persona and who are members of groups considered cultural pariahs may require more than personal psychotherapy and personal creative and spiritual practices to overcome this double legacy. Collective activities may also be necessary, such as political activism and support groups. The practice of socially disenfranchised groups gathering among themselves to form a more positive group identity has been much derided by backlash commentators as "identity politics" (for instance, women's studies programs are described in terms of their rigidity and infighting). However, such efforts are necessary to counteract the power of the culture's collective projection of Pariah-hood onto these groups. Such collective work can create room for the necessary personal work and individuation, but does not replace that work.

CHAPTER SIX

VICTIM AS TRICKSTER

Fitcher's Bird

THERE was once a wizard who used to pretend to be a beggar in order to catch pretty girls. One day he appeared before the door of a man who had three pretty daughters. The wizard carried the eldest away to his house, which stood in the midst of a dark forest. Everything in the house was magnificent; he gave her everything she could possibly desire and said, "My darling, you will certainly be happy with me, for you have everything your heart can desire." This lasted a few days, and then he said, "I must journey forth and leave you alone for a short time; here are the keys of the house; you may go everywhere and look at everything except into one room, which this little key opens, and there I forbid you to go." He likewise gave her an egg and said, "Preserve the egg carefully for me, and carry it continually about with you."

The young woman took the egg and promised to obey him in everything. When he was gone, she went all around the house from the bottom to the top and examined everything. The rooms shone with silver and gold, and she thought she had never seen such great splendor. At length she came to the forbidden door, and though she wanted to be obedient, she could have no rest until she went in. But what did she see when she entered? A great bloody basin stood in the middle of the room, and therein lay women's bodies, dead and hewn to pieces. She was so terribly alarmed that the egg, which she held in her hand, fell into the basin. She washed and scrubbed, but she could not get the blood off the egg.

It was not long before the wizard returned from his journey, and the first things he asked for were the key and the egg. She gave them to him, but she trembled as she did so, and he saw at once by the red spots that she had been in the bloody chamber. "Since you have gone into the room against my will," said he, "you shall go back into it against your own. Your life is ended." He threw her down, dragged her along by her hair, cut off her head on the block, and hewed her in pieces so that her blood ran on the ground.

Then he went back for the second daughter. He caught her like the first, by simply touching her, and carried her away. She did not fare better than her sister. Then the wizard went and brought the third sister, but she was wily. When he had given her the keys and the egg and had left, she put the egg away with great care and then examined the house, going at last into the forbidden room. Both her sisters were in the bloody basin, cruelly murdered and cut in pieces. But she began to gather their limbs together and put them in order—head, body, arms, and legs. When nothing further was wanting the limbs began to move and unite themselves together, and both the maidens were once more alive. Then they rejoiced and kissed and held one another.

The wizard returned and at once demanded the keys and the egg. When he could perceive no trace of any blood on the egg he said, "You have passed the test, you shall be my bride." He no longer had any power over her; rather, he was forced to do whatever she desired. Said she, "You shall first take a basketful of gold to my father and mother, and carry it yourself on your back; in the meantime I will prepare for the wedding." Then she ran to her sisters, whom she had hidden in a little chamber, and said, "The time has come when I can save you. The wretch himself shall take you home again, but as soon as you are at home, send help."

She put both of them in a basket and covered them over with gold, so that nothing of them was to be seen. Then she called in the wizard and said to him, "Now carry the basket away, but I shall look through my little window and watch to see if you stop." The wizard raised the basket on his back and went away with it, but it weighed him down so heavily that the sweat streamed from his face. Then he sat down to rest. But immediately one of the girls in the basket cried, "I am looking through my little window, and I see that you are resting. Go on at once!" He thought it was his bride talking to him, and he got up on his legs again. And whenever he stood still, she cried this, and then he was forced to go onward, until at last, groaning and out of breath, he took the basket with the gold and the two maidens into their parents' house.

At home the bride prepared the marriage feast and sent invitations to the friends of the wizard. Then she took a skull with grinning teeth, put some ornaments and a wreath of flowers on it, carried it upstairs to the garret window, and let it look out from thence. When all was ready, she got into a barrel of honey and then cut the featherbed open and rolled herself in it, until she looked like a wondrous bird, and no one could recognize her. Then she went out of the house, and on her way she met some of the wedding guests, who asked,

"O, Fitcher's bird, how com'st thou here?"
"I come from Fitcher's house quite near."
"And what may the young bride be doing?"
"From cellar to garret she's swept all clean,
And now from the window she's peeping, I ween."

At last she met the bridegroom, who was coming slowly back. He, like the others asked,

"O, Fitcher's bird, how com'st thou here?"
"I come from Fitcher's house quite near."
"And what may the young bride be doing?"
"From cellar to garret she's swept all clean,
And now from the window she's peeping, I ween."

The bridegroom looked up, saw the decked-out skull, thought it was his bride, and nodded to her, greeting her kindly. When he and all his guests had arrived, the bride's kinsmen, sent by her sisters, locked the doors of the house and set fire to it. The wizard and all his crew had to burn.

The wily victim is an admired figure in our popular culture. The seemingly helpless and overwhelmed prey who "gets the drop" on a predatory abuser is a form of hero. This particular adaptation to abuse can be consuming because of its cultural support, and frequently it leads to abusive behavior from the victim-trickster, who may become obsessed with acting as a nemesis to real and perceived abusers. "Fitcher's Bird," a variant of "Bluebeard," is full of scenes in which victims become tyrants and tyrants are victimized. The transmutations of the characters connect us to the profound mutability of the internal imaginal world and to the opportunity for alchemical change inherent in that mutability. The transformations involved can be so dramatic that the extremely dangerous conditions that lead to the Trickster persona are sometimes hard to see clearly.

The Trickster identity develops in a complicated family situation in which love is intimately related to violence. The child who becomes identified with a Trickster persona is "taken prisoner . . . by courtship"[1] in a home that combines intense, smothering expressions of love with out-of-control violent behavior. The Trickster internalizes the contrary unpredictability of the family's life, using it as a basis for identity and to develop a shape-shifting persona. The Trickster becomes a "moving target." Frequently he or she is the only member of the family to escape direct abuse but is forced to witness abuse and feels complicit with it. Domestic violence is at the heart of the history of every Trickster with whom I have worked. The Trickster develops an approach to life in which he or she is both provocateur and nemesis to perpetrators of abuse.

Development of the Trickster Identity

A person who develops a Trickster victim persona frequently comes from a home in which the children are left unprotected. Reading "Fitcher's Bird," we wonder if the family notices that their daughters and sisters have disappeared? No one is suspicious of this dangerous man or acts to protect these girls. In families that engender the Trickster victim identity, children are repeatedly damaged and then, alternately, given inflated, overwhelming attention. Sometimes these contradictions are acted out on the same child, sometimes children are treated differently. Meanwhile, the adults in the family behave as though everything is normal. Not surprisingly, this contradictory environment brings out the Trickster archetype in one or more of the family members. The archetypal Trickster faces both ways, toward consciousness and unconsciousness, embodying contradiction; it is both the "the archetype of the emerging ego" and "the representation of the energy flowing from the collective unconscious into consciousness."[2] The child who is to survive this family atmosphere needs that stance desperately.

Riane was the youngest of three children and her mother's favorite. As an adult she was extremely successful in a hard-driving profession that required considerable creativity. Riane was a very noticeable person, about one hundred pounds overweight and flamboyantly dressed in avant-garde style. She entered therapy because of her eating disorder and because of her insomnia. Slowly the hidden story of her family emerged. Her mother constantly abused Riane's older brother and sister, beating them, berating them, and humiliating them on a regular basis. Their father, himself often berated and denigrated by the mother, never intervened. Riane witnessed everything and, as the recipient of a maternal favoritism that was every bit as out of control as the abuse, felt horribly guilty. Her siblings suffered in childhood, and as adults, they could not care for themselves. Her sister was viciously beaten by her husband. Her brother became homeless and lived for years on the edge of survival. Riane became a Trickster, a changeling who hid behind a variety of outlandish disguises and appeared to take an ironic stance toward everything while plotting secret, indirect vengeance. Inexplicable fears and compulsions intruded on her nights.

The children in Riane's family were essentially captives, held hostage by their mother's violence. In her analysis of the dynamics of domestic captivity, Judith Herman states, "In situations of captivity, the perpetrator becomes the most powerful person in the life of the victim, and the psychology of the victim is shaped by the actions and beliefs of the perpetrator."[3] In "Fitcher's Bird" the wizard is all-powerful and no one, neither the first two sisters nor the family resists his power. This configuration reflects both a historical situation and a psychological situation in the Trickster's life. In Riane's family her mother was treated as all-powerful, and her beliefs determined the emotional life of the family. No one in the family resisted until Riane developed her Trickster identity. Riane's father witnessed the systematic demoralization of his two older children without any apparent qualms. Riane, in the meantime, was being devoured by her mother's possessiveness. This history left a legacy in the adult children of the family. Their innocence and vulnerability, the essence of their childlike trust, was split off into the unconscious. For Riane's siblings this unresolved descent manifested itself in adulthood in living situations that were abusive hells, amplified versions of their childhood experience, descents without return. They appeared to be submerged in Pariah identities. Riane was herself trapped in a victim persona of a different kind.

The sisters' captivity in the wizard's castle is a descent into an Underworld of domination, dismemberment, and death. The first two sisters go through the first stage of initiation, that is, separation from their old identities as daughters, and enter into the second stage of possibility. They explore the castle-Underworld, they encounter the shadow in visceral terms, and they undergo dismemberment. Dismemberment is, in myths of descent (see the Sumerian tale of Inanna) and in shaman's descriptions of their initiatory spirit journeys, a common precursor to transformation in the Underworld. Dismemberment can be interpreted as symbolizing a liminal state of shape-changing potential. However, the first two sisters do not return from dismemberment through their own development. They cannot reach the third stage of initiation, that of a new identity and consciousness, they cannot return from the Underworld until the "wily" sister intervenes. Why is the wily third sister necessary to this process? What keeps the first two sisters trapped in the wizard's scheme?

The wizard cannot terrorize and kill his wives without isolating, intimidating, and controlling them first. The first two sisters are completely cut off from their previous relationships. This is common in homes dominated by violence. Although the fairy tale depicts surreal circumstances, it is not so far from the everyday reality of domestic violence. As Herman states, "Perpetrators universally seek to isolate their victims. . . ."[4] Perpetrators of domestic violence in our society use "techniques of disempowerment and disconnection . . . to instill terror and helplessness . . . to destroy the victim's sense of self in relation to others."[5] Similarly, the wizard employs intimidating mannerisms, bizarre, petty rules, veiled threats, and his patriarchal authority as husband to create an enclosed atmosphere of menace. What is the typical response to this strategy? "The ultimate effect . . . is to convince the victim that the perpetrator is omnipotent, that resistance is futile, that her life depends . . . on absolute compliance."[6] Even knowing this effect of prolonged domination (sometimes called the Stockholm syndrome), we are nagged by one question when we read this fairy tale and when we read the newspaper reports of battered wives: Why can't these women see through the stratagems of intimidation and stand up for themselves?

Victims of this kind of domination tend to lose contact with their inner resources. "Captivity produces profound alterations in the victim's identity . . . . All the psychological structures of the self—the images of the body, the internalized images of others, and the values and ideals that lend a person a sense of coherence and purpose—have been invaded and systematically broken down."[7] The systematic repetitive infliction of psychological and/or physical trauma, usually followed by intermittent rewards and comforts, produces a typical response that can be seen in both political prisoners and victims of domestic violence. The victim's sense of autonomy is attacked through domination and humiliation. He or she is cut off from all sources of support and mirroring outside the abusive relationship. "In the absence of any other human connection [the captive] will try to find the humanity in her captor."[8] Generally, the victim will come to see things through the eyes of the perpetrator. The first two sisters in "Fitcher's Bird" exhibit perhaps, a common, we might even say normal, response to their situation.

In Riane's family each member was effectively prevented from forming substantive emotional relationships with anyone but Riane's mother. Her father, the only family member with the real-world power to intervene in his wife's dominating, violent oppression of the children, allowed her to completely control the atmosphere of the home. The children were kept separate from each other and from their father, both physically and emotionally. Riane's mother maintained a constant round of secret confidences with each sibling, secrets that poisoned all family connections with suspicion, and she portrayed herself as the child's only hope in a family where everyone else was untrustworthy. Hers was a concerted effort to destroy the siblings' internal sense of attachment to each other and to their father. As

Herman points out, "The destruction of attachments requires not only the isolation of the victim from others but also the destruction of her internal images of connection to others."[9]

Being held captive and being controlled by an abusive authority produces "protracted depression, hyper-arousal, insomnia, nightmares, psychosomatic complaints, dissociation, paralysis of initiative," even in adults, such as political prisoners, who have developed identities before their captivity.[10]

As has been documented in many prolonged hostage situations and in battered spouse syndrome, it is normal for passivity and constriction of activity to set in, sometimes amounting to the loss of the will to live. This is a reality that backlash commentators, in their attachment to the hero persona, are loath to acknowledge. In children who have known no life outside domestic captivity the effects are more severe. Children raised in this way most often carry a deeply embedded, rarely articulated belief that slavish obedience is necessary not only to survival but also to lovability, that the only way to be loved is to obliterate the self. It is not hard to see why the first two sisters in "Fitcher's Bird" or Riane's older siblings responded in the normal way, with learned helplessness and paralysis. The more difficult, and perhaps more productive, question to ask is: How does the third sister manage to respond differently? What psychological capacities are embodied in this wily sister?

The third sister is a Trickster. Jung describes the archetypal Trickster as having "a fondness for sly jokes, and miraculous pranks, power as a shape-shifter, a dual nature, part animal, a tendency to expose himself to torture and an approximation to the figure of a savior."[11] We can easily see these traits in the third daughter. She is sly, as evidenced by her trick with the egg; her pranks include fooling the wizard into laboriously carrying her sisters home and dressing up the skeleton as a bride. She is a shape-shifter who appears as an animal, the bird made of honey and feathers. She is in danger of torture and death throughout the story, and she is her sisters' savior. Riane enjoyed tricking people and approached even straightforward interaction with a sly twist. She used her clothes and ever-changing weight to constantly change shape and appearance. She seemed to seek out torturous and difficult work situations. She desperately wanted to save her family.

Witnessing and Resisting

Riane's relatives inevitably saw Riane as a pampered mama's girl and resented her for her apparent privilege. Meanwhile, her inner experience was one of being overwhelmed by the horror of what she was witnessing and of being forced to be intimate with someone who was clearly dangerous. Riane was not psychologically dismembered, as were her brother and sister, but she was still living in the wizard's castle, with its constant threat of torture and terror. Riane was in the position of the third sister who enters the bloody chamber and witnesses the annihilation of her siblings. She became the tyrant's beloved: "You have stood the test, you shall be my bride," the wizard says to the third sister. And, like the third sister, Riane responded with an outer facade of compliance coupled with an inner resistance.

Children who develop a Trickster persona are adept at altered states of consciousness. They become internal shape-shifters. All children employ altered states both to play and to defend themselves against the internal effects of experiences that might otherwise be intolerable. States of dissociation are available to all children. These include: living in a fantasy world; derealization, a state in which events do not feel real; depersonalization, a state in which the child does not experience himself or herself as real; and time relativity, a state in which time speeds up or alternatively stands still. Most adults remember such states of consciousness as part of the magic of childhood and the freedom of play. This may account for many of the "lost paradise" images we have of childhood in general. The abused child needs to use these trance states both to "disappear" internally from horrific, inescapable events and to preserve some part of the Self, to try to keep some aspect of inner life uncontaminated by an intrusive and unwholesome family environment. The more extreme the environment, the more adept the child becomes at altered consciousness. The bizarre transformations of the fairy tale in which the Trickster turns herself into a bird or presents a skeleton as a bride are symbolic representations of this type of inner transformation of experience. As with the Pariah persona, the Trickster is forced by the destructiveness of her environment to retreat deep into the archetypal realm for the tools of survival. No human agency is willing or able to proffer help. This results in a magical, surreal persona that seems set apart from normal human interaction. The archetype of the Trickster begins to inform adaptation, promoting small rebellions through pranks and provocations, many of them subtle, some of them blatant.

In a tyrannical environment small, subtle gestures, which

may appear pointless, can serve to maintain the inner experience of autonomy and ultimately aid in larger changes.[12] In "Fitcher's Bird" the third sister's first act of defiance seems trivial, not worth the risk. She puts the egg safely aside, even though at this point in the story she cannot know its telltale significance. This is simply a gesture of autonomy, a refusal to allow the wizard-tyrant to control her mind, even though he controls her physical reality. It is important that this is a conscious gesture of resistance, a choice rather than a compulsive, unconscious rebellion such as the impulse that overwhelms her compliant sisters and causes them to enter the forbidden room. These gestures are crucial, and their importance is rarely understood. They preserve an inner spark of autonomy and represent the refusal to bond completely with the aggressor—the refusal to acquiesce internally to one's own betrayal. Deliberately preserving inner images of the Self as having some choices is vital to psychological survival and is crucial to developing and maintaining an internal reflective space that is not dominated by the aggressor. Sometimes this is all that these small gestures accomplish; at other times the small gestures build to a large-scale change, as they do in the fairy tale. Riane's first memories were of silently saying to herself "I love my sister," when her mother was on a rampage against her older sister. This did nothing practical for the sister at that moment, of course, but it expressed Riane's resistance to identifying completely with her mother's domination and dictation of reality. Riane was only a child herself, and so, inevitably, she went back and forth in this stance for a long time, alternately identifying with and separating from her mother's sadistic behavior. Over time Riane developed a repertoire of small internal and external gestures, most of them consisting of silent acknowledgments of feeling, which were signals to herself that she had some choices. In stressful and difficult circumstances people often respond to questions about their feelings by saying, "What does it matter how I feel? That won't change anything." In fact, asserting the importance of one's own responses despite the circumstances—treating the feelings as a reality that can transcend the circumstances—changes one's experience of oneself and provides an internal boundary.

Riane was in the family role that seems most likely to produce the Trickster persona—that of the witness who is spared. As such she had the opportunity to observe the abusive dysfunction of the family without having her capacity to observe and reflect overwhelmed by physical and emotional assault. She developed a consciousness of the shadow side of the family's life that other family members did not have. At the same time she had to go along outwardly with her mother's favoritism toward herself, much as the wily sister pretends to be willing to marry the wizard and prepares for a wedding she does not intend to complete. For Riane this situation produced a kind of double consciousness, a tricksterish tendency to shape-shift. This double consciousness allowed her to outwardly accommodate her mother's domination while preserving a private, secret inner life. In abusive, tyrannical situations that cannot be escaped, failure to develop this double consciousness means that one will either bring down annihilation on oneself through open resistance or lose one's inner self to the domination of the tyrant. Riane was playful with her mother, which gave the entire family moments of relief and allowed Riane some feeling of power and impact. It also left her with considerable survivor's guilt and the unconscious belief that she should be able to save the family.

The third sister is the first and, in the life of the story, the only family member to become aware of the wizard's shadow nature and remain alive, that is, conscious. As soon as the first two sisters encounter the shadow they are overwhelmed by it and die. Consequently, the wily sister is the only one who has the opportunity to save her sisters from his shadow side. Jung says, regarding the Trickster as savior, "The recognition and unavoidable integration of the shadow creates such a harrowing situation that nobody but a savior can undo the tangled web of fate."[13]

This was true in Riane's family and in her psyche; within her family she was the conscious witness of the dysfunction that the other family members were overwhelmed by, and outside the family, she was especially aware of the dark side of life. This special connection to the shadow served her well in the family. Her Tricksterish playfulness helped her maintain the intimacy with her mother that was necessary to survival. At the same time, playfulness gave her some ironic distance from that smothering connection. Her reliance on mild trance states, including those brought on by compulsive, ritualistic binge eating, helped her preserve some inner space of privacy and aided her in maintaining her chameleon-like outer facade. Her secret acts of defiance helped her develop and preserve a sense of internal independence and identity. As is usually the case, the same coping mechanisms that promoted survival within the family and, because of their survival value, became embedded in the ego's approach to life, were a liability in the world outside the family. In fact, these coping mechanisms serve frequently to re-create the family dynamics in situations that could be different. By the time Riane entered therapy, the true Self was so well hidden that she could not find it.

Attachment to the Trickster Identity

Repetition compulsion in the Trickster's life story tends to be both striking in its blatancy and difficult to confront in its self-destructive aspects. Typically the Trickster seeks out situations that are unnecessarily oppressive and then works hard to slyly turn them on end. She appears to unconsciously perceive herself as a type of nemesis to oppressive authority.

Riane played out this scenario in her working life. She was successful in a profession that required great creativity and in which she could make excellent use of her chameleon-like social skills, taking on the emotional color of whomever she needed to influence. She had a good reputation in her field and changed jobs fairly frequently, each time ostensibly for higher pay and broader horizons. However, each new job presented her with an intolerably oppressive situation that had to be rectified. As I got to know Riane, I began to sense that she was drawn to such situations and that when she had a choice among potential jobs, as frequently happened, she would choose one in which she knew some authority problem existed. On those occasions when no such obvious problem existed, she uncovered one. Riane would then have the opportunity to play out her persona-establishing rapport with the oppressive authority figure while working behind the scenes to disrupt the system and turn it around in favor of those she saw as oppressed.

Each time she went through one of these cycles she felt heroic, and her long-festering survivor's guilt was assuaged for a short period of time. Her guilt, however irrational, at being the only child in her family who was not openly abused was a driving though unacknowledged force in her inner life. As her siblings' adult lives fell apart while she became more successful, this dynamic increased in intensity. When her sister married a violent man, guilt became Riane's primary unconscious motivation. Her inability to save her brother and sister was experienced, in an unexamined way, as an unwillingness to save them. When she looked at her childhood, Riane could not see herself as a true child, that is, as a dependent family member without the power to determine the family's structure.

There were several reasons for this distortion. First, Riane had fallen for the family legend of herself as the favored one, and she had little conscious awareness of the destructive effects of the family dynamics on herself. Second, she had an inflated sense of her own impact on things. This came from her mother's incessant, narcissistically motivated grandiose praise, and it also came from her connection to the archetypal Trickster. This uncontained connection to the archetype caused an ego inflation. Third, Riane was deeply attached to her savior fantasies, as they related to family, friends, and colleagues. In order to be a savior she could not afford to think of her own wounds. Finally, Riane's experience of her own vulnerable, innocent, and exploited child aspect was obscured by her forced identification with the aggressor, her mother.

The Internalized Tyrant and the Dismembered Shadow

As in our discussion of Beauty and the Beast, we see that the Trickster has a special relationship to the family shadow. Like the Redeemer, the Trickster is the one who can deal with the dangerous parent and navigate, outwardly, the dangerous waters of the family's pathology. The particular nature of the family relationships, however, creates not a shadow beast like the Redeemer's but an ego identification with the aggressor. The Trickster persona rests on a heroic ego ideal that is modeled on the aggressive, dominating tactics of the family tyrant, tactics that are indirectly supported by the culture's valorization of control and power. Despite the Trickster's efforts to resist bonding completely with the aggressor, she must identify with at least one parent as a part of ego development and that parent will more likely be the stronger one, even given that stronger parent's sadism. The Trickster is split within herself, unconsciously resisting and unconsciously emulating the tyrant. This is the internalized reflection of the double consciousness used by the Trickster in her external dealings with authority figures, in which she both identifies with and resists them. The internal tyrant is offset by a shadow that embodies the dismembered innocent, trusting, and powerless child, trapped in the Underworld of the bloody chamber. The loss of that innocence, coming about as the result of having to witness abuse, may result in considerable bitterness.

This internal configuration means that the adult Trickster is often experienced by others as something of a tyrant, even while experiencing herself as a savior. The Trickster may be unconscious of her own cruelty. The compulsion to outwit and fool the oppressor operates both in truly oppressive situations and in benign situations. Obviously, in benign situations someone must be made into, that is, perceived as, an oppressor and then tricked. In all situations the Trickster sees herself as the sole reliable source of assessing things. This is a legacy of the family situation of being the only conscious witness of the family shadow, the only person in touch with that reality. Taken together these *modi operandi* mean that in relationships the Trickster is frequently experienced as a charismatic but overbearing handful, a busybody who is prone to vendettas that may or may not be justified. Her unconscious identification with the family tyrant and her inner perception that her power is being used to save others make it very difficult for her to perceive the problem in her own behavior. Her deep suspicion of perceptions other than her own makes it difficult for others to reflect their experience of her persona back to her. The Trickster often communicates the repressed shadow dimensions of her experience through a passive-into-active process. She assumes the active role in interpersonal drama when formerly she had been forced into the passive role. She unconsciously puts others in the position she was in as a child—that of the helpless witness. She does this through direct and indirect pressure, both verbal and nonverbal. Riane would stage intense confrontations with her boss in front of co-workers, failing to understand their distress, since her position was righteous.

The internalized tyrant is bound up with the Trickster persona as part of the ego and also operates in the Trickster's relationship to herself. The Trickster's relationship to herself as well as to others tends toward the tyrannical. Internal dialogue is often pressured and overbearing.

Riane's attempts to parent herself, to reflect on or modify her own behavior, took place through self-righteous criticism of a searing, absolutist nature. The voice was unconsciously modeled on her mother's.

The Trickster-identified person keeps all the vulnerable aspects of the Self carefully set aside. Riane had a nighttime self. At night she would be overcome by physical tension, hyper-arousal, fear, and something bordering on despair. She suffered from severe insomnia, and occasionally she experienced the collapse of all initiative. The life her siblings lived openly she lived in secret. Riane experienced her shadow as a contaminated aspect of identity, and she viewed it with shame and self-loathing. It was the innocent, trusting child in her that had been dismembered by the abuse she had witnessed and by the smothering, intrusive attention that had been forced upon her. Her rage and hatred, when not directed against oppressive bosses, was directed against herself for being vulnerable to wounding, for not being strong enough to conquer her mother. This was a by-product of her heroic stance and a form of victim blaming. Her shame increased her tendency to be a "moving target" within intimate relationships. The dismembered shadow child needed to be discovered, reconstructed, and re-animated.

Resurrection of the Sisters

As I mentioned at the beginning of this chapter, "Fitcher's Bird" is a variation of the fairy tale motif known as "Bluebeard." In that better known version the wizard is named Bluebeard; the story focuses on only one woman's story, rather than three; and the abductee is rescued in the end entirely by family members rather than by her own acts. The inclusion of the two sisters in our story and the different ending are significant (we will address that ending later). The sisters reflect an important part of the Trickster's personal psyche and also symbolize the dismemberment of the feminine by the domination of certain cultural values. Both of these levels need to be addressed by the Trickster in order to pursue her individuation.

For Riane, certain talents and pleasures had been torn apart by their association with the destructive dynamics of her family. Her natural leanings toward art and toward athletics had been taken over by her mother's grandiose narcissism and had been used to belittle her siblings through comparison. As a consequence, Riane could take no pleasure in either talent, and as soon as she left home she stopped these activities. Riane's liminal capacity, her considerable medial connection to the unconscious, had been taken over by the family's pathological needs. Her playfulness and her inner reflective space were fragmented by the way they had been used to help her survive in a violent environment. To reclaim these aspects of her Self, Riane needed to reanimate the innocent, childlike parts of herself, the parts that were analogous to the dismembered sisters. The vulnerable shadow aspect that was rendered unconscious and dismembered by what she had witnessed needed attention. A direct part of this re-membering was literal remembering, a conscious reconstructing of the abusive events of childhood. Denial, complicated by Riane's use of altered states, made this reconstruction of history slow and uneven. But, for the Trickster, remembering both the events and the emotional response to them is crucial.

The first two sisters in "Fitcher's Bird" represent a kind of innocence that cannot survive in a place like the wizard's castle or like Riane's family. The Trickster differs from her "sisters" in that, after her innocent, trusting childish potential is betrayed and trapped in the bloody chamber, she retains the playful, liminal aspect of childhood and builds her Trickster persona upon it. In order to reclaim the full potential of the Self she must revisit the bloody chamber; that is, she must recall the damage done by past abuse. She must reassemble the dismembered sisters, which means recalling and recathecting the innocent, childlike part of herself that was betrayed and shattered by what she witnessed. And finally, she must reanimate that trusting part.

The issue of revivifying trust is a tricky one, and it connects with the second level of the symbolism of the sisters. In order to be free of the victim persona, trust must be regained. But the family circumstances that made innocent trust dangerous and wiliness wise are all too often encountered in daily life. As Jessica Benjamin points out in *The Bonds of Love,* her comprehensive psychological analysis of the problem of domination in Western culture, abusive authority is common in our culture, and its psychological underpinnings are intimately connected to the Western worldview.[14] That worldview tends to denigrate vulnerability as weakness and to valorize power. This means that our culture tolerates domineering behavior, especially when the victim of domination is perceived as deserving of or needing domination. The Trickster can find recreations of her family situation on every talk show.

The Trickster is simultaneously confronted with a personal and a philosophical problem. She has witnessed evil and abusive acts, she may have participated in them, however tricksterishly, and she sees them recreated in the news every day. Consequently, "her moral ideals must coexist with knowledge of the capacity for evil, both within others and within herself."[15] The Trickster must build a safe container of trustworthy relationships for herself that are carefully assessed, based not on blind childlike trust but on conscious knowledge that evil exists and must be taken into account. Within such a container the Trickster can experiment with bringing trust back to life. In the family of most Tricksters trust leads to annihilation, but at the same time the alternative, wiliness, leads to a loss of authenticity in relationships. The resurrection of the sisters, the reclaiming of trust, is the beginning of the third stage of initiation, the development of an identity that expands beyond the role dictated by the family crucible.

I have called the cultural aspect of the sisters' dismemberment and reanimation a problem for the feminine. By this I mean that, as in our discussion of the gender implications of the story of the rape of Persephone, the qualities of innocent, trusting vulnerability tend to be embodied in feminine imagery. Images of overpowering tyranny and piercing domination tend to be masculine. This means that for many people, perhaps the majority of those raised in Western culture, escaping the internalized tyrant means transforming an aspect of the Self that seems masculine and resurrecting the trust and vulnerability that we associate with the feminine.

This genderized split is reflected in outer social realities. In the vast majority of cases of domestic violence the perpetrators of violent domination are men and the adult victims are women. Gender-role conditioning is an active factor in this phenomenon. Control and power are associated with the masculine gender-role as positive traits, just as yielding softness is associated with the feminine role as a positive trait. The accompanying shadow traits, domination in the masculine and passivity in the feminine, are inevitably associated with gender roles as well. This means that one is more likely to find men who are domestic tyrants and women who are the passive victims of such domination. Riane's sister was one such woman. She married an abusive, homicidal man. Her experiences with her mother left her with no model or motivation for self-protection, and so she was easily susceptible to a man whose desire was to dominate and dismember. Indeed, if she was like most abused children, her childhood experiences, taken together with the fact that extended family and society treated those experiences as acceptable, probably left her with the unarticulated belief that this was the life she deserved.

In addition, "Since most women derive pride and self-esteem from their capacity to sustain relationships, the batterer is often able to entrap his victim by appealing to her most cherished values."[16] That is, a battered woman often sees the relationship as more important than herself. In a nonabusive situation this can be a tremendous strength, allowing women to effectively foster relationships. In an abusive situation it can be a death sentence. In the case of Riane's sister, as with so many battered women, personal and family history made her susceptible to abuse while cultural expectations of women enforced exactly those experiences that made her vulnerable. Society provided her with little or no collective wisdom with which she, as a woman, might counteract her individual conditioning in the family. The sudden arrival of "kinsmen" who burn the wizard at the end of "Fitcher's Bird" may be related to these aspects of gender role conditioning: The final resolution of captivity requires the intervention, on behalf of the vulnerable aspects of the Self, of an assertive part that our culture defines as masculine.

An important aspect of Riane's work included consciously holding her brother's and sister's fates in her mind, including their source in their shared history, rather than suppressing the memory as she had previously done. It was also important to make direct, as opposed to indirect—Tricksterish—overtures to her siblings. Riane began to develop a vital sense of shared experience that she was able to extend outside the family. This was the beginning of the end of a long exile for her. Her identification with the Trickster victim persona had cut her off from seeing her experiences as part of the common vicissitudes of human life, experiences that should and could be shared with others. Riane began to seek relationships in which authenticity and mutual recognition were possible. She also began to revalue the parts of herself that she had denigrated as too feminine. This was an internal and external resurrection of the sisters.

After the sisters are resurrected, the wily sister fools the wizard into believing that she has obeyed him. She begins to be able to use the power of the tyrant to change things, to bring the sisters home—that is, to bring the shadow aspects back into consciousness. Her conscious effort to use power on behalf of herself and her sisters begins to loosen the internalized tyrant's hold and to disentangle the transformative power of the Trickster's liminal gifts from being identified with the aggressor. The ego must see the tyrannical impulse for what it is—bullying—and be willing to use the mind's abilities to thwart internalized domination. The Trickster's unacknowledged connection with the internalized tyrant needs to be addressed and to be consciously challenged in internal dialogue.

For Riane this meant noticing the many times she heard the overbearing, self-righteous tone of her mother's voice in her interactions both with other people and with herself. She then had to consciously challenge the legitimacy of that tone. Learning to observe her internal commentary without automatically judging it and then learning to assess the effects of that commentary on herself and others slowed Riane's compulsive behavior down. When this begins to happen the power of the Trickster's connection to the archetypal level can be used in service of her own individuation rather than in service of repetition compulsion. The wizard's power begins to change hands. Psychologically, this is a recollecting of power from its projection onto the abuser. Power begins to be explored within the self and is no longer experienced exclusively as a property of others. This takes place during a time when external danger has passed, when the ego has learned how to make safe, non-abusive relationships, and it becomes possible to grapple with the psychological legacy of domination. Riane's mother, for example, had real power over her children, and through years of domination she acquired psychological power over their inner lives. Her children, as adults, continued to project that psychological power onto their mother and onto others, even though as adults they could have power of their own. Some of the people they projected this power onto were also tyrants, others were demonized by the projection. These projections sapped the adult children of their own experience of psychological power. The reclamation of power requires becoming conscious of the projection. The conscious exercise of choice stops the repetition compulsion in its tracks.

Transformation

Speaking of the Trickster archetype, Ron Messer states, "The Trickster can serve as a gateway back to the revivifying aspects of the unconscious, which can renew and regenerate conscious life."[17] As the ego-work on the internalized tyrant and the shadow-work of bringing to light the dismembered innocence proceed, this gateway aspect of the Trickster begins to guide individuation. The very legacy of abuse that produces the victim identity can provide a threshold to the storehouse of transformative images residing in the unconscious. This does not mean that the abuse that Riane, for example, suffered as a child was good for her, merely that the cycle of disintegration can turn to integration, that the seeds of resolution for an initiatory descent may lie in the heart of its effects. This is essentially an alchemical process, cyclical not linear, where dualistic categories blend and merge into one. The process happens in the following way.

As the wily sister experiences her power to transform her circumstances and herself, her consciousness changes. Within the container of the wizard's house the third sister experiences the resurrection of that which was lost; she confronts the bloody shadow and grapples with it. She is coming into relationship with the unconscious, moving consciously through the Underworld. "The situation is now gradually illumined as is a dark night by a rising moon. . . . This dawning light corresponds to the albedo." The albedo is an alchemical concept referring to an intermediate, transformative stage in the endless natural cycle of destruction (called negredo) and growth (called rubedo). It is "not a sharply circumscribed world with clear forms but a consciousness of imagination . . . an intermediate realm between bright, clear, daylight and pitch-black night; the mediumistic world where one thing can also be another. . . ."[18] It is a Tricksterish entrance to increased consciousness, and as such it depends a great deal on liminality; it is a betwixt and between state that allows access to the unconscious and mediates between internal dualisms. In this case the opposites of victim and hero, bride and murderer, coexist within the same figure.

The path to increased consciousness for the wily sister begins with an egg. Putting away the egg is the first act of conscious resistance to the tyrant. It continues with exploration and the discovery of the dismembered parts of the Self, the sisters. Those parts are reanimated, and the power of the tyrant is used to bring them home, back into consciousness. Consciousness of the true nature of things continues to be expressed when the third sister dresses the skeleton as a bride, for of course she is the one who finally realizes that all of the wizard's brides are dead. All unions with the internalized tyrant end in loss of consciousness. Finally she fulfills the promise of the egg and finds freedom as a wondrous bird. The egg is the potential for true development, which cannot come to full bloom under captivity.

The wondrousness and magical quality of the third sister's exit from the wizard's domain reflects the power of the evolving Self. Escaping as a bird flaunts the freedom and joy of the emerging Self. Inspiration emerges when the ego is more influenced by the Self. Riane's playful talent for perceiving the unseen side of things and her great creative flexibility began to blossom in new directions after she began to dismantle her identification with the aggressor. In trusting relationships and without the drain of repetition compulsion, her energy poured out in free expression—art, work, and social life all reflected this change.

This is a part of what is symbolized by the conflagration of the wizard and his cronies. An outburst of energy, which may well be fiery, accompanies the deconstruction of the internalized tyrant. This deconstruction is the mirror image of the reconstruction of the sisters, of the innocent shadow. Strength and assertiveness can begin to manifest in helpful forms, like the kinsmen of the story's ending, rather than through either an unconscious identification with or projection of the tyrant. The various compulsive defenses that had served to keep the internal configuration of internalized tyrant and dismembered shadow in place begin to lose their grip. In Riane's case, her compulsive eating became treatable. She was finally willing to attend Overeater's Anonymous and, with group support and a sponsor, she eventually lost one hundred pounds.

The narrative of transformation in "Fitcher's Bird" helps us see the journey through the Underworld more clearly. The wily sister negotiates the dark realm of death and becomes, in a way, a Queen of the Underworld. She becomes adept at descending and returning, able to retain consciousness in the face of the deepest shadow, artful and humorous in her response to events. Humor can be touchy for people who are trying to disidentify from a victim persona. Ridicule presented as humor is frequently used to invalidate the victim's experience, on both personal and societal levels. Reclaiming humor, beginning to discern the difference between denigration and funniness, is crucial to deconstructing a victim identity. The phenomenon of humorlessness is often noted in activist groups. This humorless stage, in which everything is minutely examined and analyzed for signs of disrespect, does not have to be permanent. It is a compensating reaction to past denial and disguising of abuse—both internal denial and collective denial. If individuation proceeds, humor returns. It is possible to see this progression in relationship to the feminist movement in which widely popular, feminist comics such as Roseanne or Brett Butler began to emerge once women's social inequality began to be recognized and admitted on a broad scale. It may be that humor can return only after recognition has been reclaimed.

The images of alchemical transformation that resolve the story of "Fitcher's Bird" reflect the personal and transpersonal power of art. Jung believed that art can provide access to profound realities that are excluded from conscious life and worldview. "In works of art of this nature . . . it cannot be doubted that the vision is a genuine primordial experience. . . . It is not something derived or secondary, it is not symptomatic of something else, it is a true symbol—that is an expression for something real but unknown."[19] The process of creating art requires the artist to bridge ego and archetype in her own psyche. The archetypes, which are the

DNA of the mythic aspect of the unconscious, engender images. These images may enable us to consider the nature of experience and our relationship to it, to express something about complex human situations like that facing the victim without reifying those situations, hardening them into polarized, rigid stances. The resulting artwork may be capable of doing something similar for the art viewer, bridging the split between ego and archetype in his or her psyche. Much of the psychological commentary on art springs from a Freudian view of symbolic material and portrays the artwork as a symbolic working through of the artist's personal conflicts. From the Jungian point of view, that is only one psychological aspect of art; the other aspects are related to visionary experience. Art making can provide a transpersonal container for the profoundly mixed experiences of those who are disidentifying from victim personae. The image of the "wondrous bird" walking down the road embodies the transpersonal aspect. There are obviously any number of ordinary methods and disguises the wily sister could use in her final escape. Her choice of a fantastical, whimsical transformation into feathers and honey illuminates the joy and creativity that spring from the Self.

CHAPTER SEVEN

PERSEPHONE RETURNS

Transforming Victim Identities

Every day we encounter circumstances, people, and experiences that leave us feeling helpless. In some situations we really are without power; some relationships exhibit real differences in power. When abuses of such power are denied, victimization is perpetuated. In other situations an internal feeling of helplessness produces powerlessness. An automatic assumption of victimhood will produce victimization even when an external abuse of power does not exist. This is the psychological reality that I have tried to explore through myth and fairy tale.

In the myth of Persephone's descent and return the archetypal roles are clearly delineated. The betrayed innocent, the ruthless abductor, the faithful rescuer, the heartless authority figure, the mediating friends are all separately embodied in a drama of transformation. Likewise, the realms of Upperworld and Underworld are, at the beginning of the myth, strictly separated. The distinctness of the myth's structure helped me to clarify the component parts of the victim's descent and return. Demeter's Upperworld journey of betrayal, grief, and reclamation was clear. The one thing that was left unclear in Persephone's story was her experience in the Underworld. Persephone's journey through the Underworld, her stages of movement from Kore to Queen of the Underworld, were vague. Working on the fairy tales has helped to clarify the areas of vagueness in the myth.

In the fairy tales, which inhabit an intermediate zone between the everyday human world and the archetypal, transformative world, roles and realms alike are more entangled and more combined. Thus the Beast in "Beauty and the Beast" plays Hades's abductor role and then also comes to embody lost aspects of the Self that need to be remembered and reclaimed. Similarly, the magical estates that each fairy tale's protagonist journeys to are Underworlds of danger and captivity and, at the same time, containers where new kinds of relationships can form, crucibles that enable each protagonist to transform an old victim identity into a new experience of the personal and transpersonal Self. The mixed images in the fairy tales have proven to be helpful for two reasons: first, psychological life as it is lived presents the same entanglements and combinations of destructive and constructive elements as the fairy tales do, and, second, the intermingling of Upperworld and Underworld in the fairy tales begins to give us more insight into the Underworld aspect of the victim's journey, a more vivid picture than we were able to see in the myth of Persephone.

Symbols of a Mixed Reality

"Symbols mediate between the unrepresentable archetypes and the world of the manifest. They link the dark realm of indefinite power, vitality, and mystery to the well-lit world of ego-consciousness with its relatively fixed meanings and limitations."[1]

Why is symbolic dialogue important to the dynamics of victim identification? It is easy for me to imagine a reductionistic, pseudo-pragmatic commentary on the approach to victim identification described in this book. It would sound something like: "This is self-indulgent and unnecessary. The situation is straightforward. All the victims need to do is . . ." This commentary could come from either camp in the victim debate, one side advocating that all the victim-identified need to do is take care of themselves and stop whining, the other side claiming that what the victim-identified really need to do is demand a legal or social intervention designed to more completely protect them from what they find hurtful.

It is important to realize two things: (1) no external change of law or mores will free an individual from internal identification with a victim persona. The rectification of oppressive laws and mores is incredibly important and it creates a context more conducive to psychological change, but it does not automatically create psychological change in an individual; and (2) a common-sense critique will not disrupt a victim persona. This is true whether the critique comes from within, consisting of the person's own self-criticism, or from without. It is true whether the critique focuses on the source of the victim identity (as in, "These injuries are not serious enough to be upset about") or on the form of behavior the victim identity engenders ("Okay, what happened to you was bad but this is an overreaction"). Such critiques will evoke anger or shame in those who are identified with a victim persona but will not dislodge the victim persona. These facts are deeply disappointing to both camps in the victim debate. The psychological reality of the victim identity requires us to grapple with both the conscious, pragmatic part of the psyche, the ego that tends to favor concrete solutions like the ones listed above, and the unconscious aspect of the psyche, where the agenda is rather different. Symbols mediate between the conflicting agendas of ego and unconscious.

The unconscious is both personal and collective, or as I have been saying, transpersonal. The personal unconscious consists of repressed memories, feelings, preferences, and capacities. This repressed material springs from the individual experiences of life with which, for a variety of reasons, the ego will not or cannot form a conscious relationship. The transpersonal level of the unconscious plugs into the archetypal power of collective human potential and is a storehouse of undeveloped resources for the individual. When someone is victimized the personal trauma of the experience leaves a legacy of conflict and wounding in the personal unconscious. It also activates the archetypal levels of the unconscious, the multifaceted images and patterns of descent, transformation, and return. The personal pain and horror of the betrayal is bound up with the transformative archetypal core.

This is both good news and bad news. It seems to be a common desire in American culture to find a way to resolve the legacy of hurtful experience without working through the messy feelings. The bad news is: the structure of the unconscious means that this will never work. The personal shadow of vulnerability, pain, and betrayal is inextricably bound up with, indeed serves as an entrance to, the part of the unconscious that provides inner guidance for the transformation of victim personae. The good news is: working on the legacy of victimizing trauma can bring one into contact with resources in the psyche that were previously inaccessible. When the youth who set out to learn what fear was enters the haunted castle it is a hellish, intensified re-creation of the experiences he has already suffered through, including an encounter with a demeaning, contemptuous old man like his father. However, when the youth fully engages with this version of the Underworld he comes to the treasure house in its depths and, as a result, eventually fulfills his quest. In this way the haunted castle reflects the structure of the unconscious.

This is the psychological complexity inherent in the structure of the psyche that the current victim discourse does not address. Absolutist concepts, exemplified by the processes of demonization and beatification, simply cannot reflect the phenomenology of this mixed reality. Understanding both the effects of identifying with a victim persona and the necessary response to such an identification requires that we appreciate the ways in which opposites like guilt and innocence are psychologically interwoven. Individual people do not embody archetypal absolutes. Victims tend to be innocent in some ways, guilty in others. Heroes tend to be saviors in some ways, tyrants in others. Images that spring from archetypal stories, from dreams, from art, and from reverie can provide a container that holds the complexity without resorting to absolutism or reification. Symbols of the mixed reality of victim identity are entrances to the deep resources of the Self. The deep resources of the Self can compensate for the distorting grip of victim personae without resorting to stultifying ideology.

Relationships: Intrapsychic and Interpersonal

"The psychic totality, the self, is a combination of opposites. Without a shadow even the self is not real."[2] The relationship between the ego, which for most people is the acknowledged "I," and the unconscious is typically dominated by what Jung calls the shadow problem. The shadow, the personal experiences, feelings, and attributes that are most inimical to the ego ideal, sits at the entrance to the unconscious, like the paralyzing river Styx at the entrance to the Underworld. In order to gain access to the inner guidance and resources of the Self through symbolic dialogue with the unconscious, the ego must come to a *modus vivendi* with the shadow. Traditional Jungian theory holds that images of the shadow are always of the same gender as the ego. I think that the stories we have been working with show us something different for issues of victim identification. The victim protagonists here are struggling with the shadow of the hero persona—the abusive tyrant. Like the hero persona itself the shadow-abuser in Western culture is associated with the masculine gender role and with masculine imagery.

Every person has a shadow and every culture has a shadow. Contemporary victim narratives are part of an important commentary on our culture's shadow, which I will address in the next chapter. The personal shadow is of course affected by the cultural shadow, but it must be worked through by each individual. No cultural or societal change will relieve an individual of this or her shadow problem. In an adult the relationships between parts of the Self, such as the ego and the shadow, are internalized, embedded. Conscious effort must be made to shift those relationships. As has been discussed in the context of the myths and fairy tales, the ego's stance toward the Self is unconsciously modeled on the parents' stance toward the child's emerging individuality. The ego's stance toward the shadow, which guides the intrapsychic relationship between ego and shadow, is more specifically based on the parents' attitude toward those aspects of the child that the parents found troublesome, unlikable, or inconvenient or that they simply did not notice or know how to respond to. These parts of the Self had to be dismissed and disdained by the child so that she could fulfill a role in the family's system. The individual's internalized stance toward the shadow, modeled on familial attitudes, must shift. When it does, the ego and the shadow come into a new relationship, a relationship that gives the ego greater access to the Self.

Internal freedom from a victim identity hinges on the willingness of the individual to observe his or her inner process. The style or tone of that self-observance must be one that furthers individuation. In listening to others talk about themselves we notice their tone—the friend whose every minor misstep brings on a flood of vicious self-criticism, the co-worker who blandly minimizes even the most obvious emotions, the relative who is always confused about her own opinion. It is possible and necessary to begin to listen for the tone of one's own inner voice. The tone of voice used in talking to oneself is powerful; it sets the atmosphere of self-observation as surely as external tone of voice determines the atmosphere of a conversation between two people. It is vital to focus on the tone of voice that ones uses in talking to oneself—to delineate, particularize, and even name the tone—so that one no longer automatically accepts it as inevitable or natural. Normally the tone of the inner voice varies, as does the outer. However, when the ego is dominated by a particular persona the tone of the inner voice is one-dimensional, always the same, determined by the ego's identification with that persona.

If the shadow is explored within an internal atmosphere of suspicion, disgust, hostility, impatience, contempt, dismissiveness, or fear, then the experience of encountering the unconscious will not challenge or balance conscious life. Instead, the product of inner exploration will pass through the filter of the ego's unchallenged attitude and will inevitably support that attitude. The most blatant example of this discussed in previous chapters was the Seeker's contempt, the self-loathing expressed by Daryl. If the voice of inner commentary is saturated with contempt, then the exploration of the shadow merely provides new material for contempt. The symbolic communications of the Self have little impact once they are filtered and skewed by the lens of a victim-identified ego.

A practical indication that the relationship between ego and shadow is being skewed and filtered by a problematic ego attitude is that self-exploration is repetitive. In other words, when an inner experience—a feeling, reaction, or image—is given conscious attention, the process always comes to the same conclusion. The end result may be cognitive or emotional. For example, whenever Sula, identified with the betrayed innocent persona, observed her own process, she noticed only faults and then tried to make plans to fix them. If she couldn't think of such a plan she would become very depressed. The content of her self-reflection was very different in each instance—at one time a dream image, at another time a relationship pattern—but the pragmatic and emotional consequences of the process were always more or less the same, that is, a plan, depression, or both. The insight and experience available through her inner work were passing through the filter of a habitual ego attitude, the product in this instance of identifying with the victim persona of the betrayed innocent. For all victim-identified, only those aspects of the symbolic dialogue that support the victim identification are held as significant by the ego and the unconscious is blocked in its compensatory purpose.

What does the process of changing the ego's attitude look like? How do people begin to alter their stance toward the shadow, the unconscious, and thus to the Self? How does an adult develop a style of self-observation, of reflection, that is progressive, that furthers individuation rather than reinforces the victim identification? The short answer to these questions is—through relationships. Just as the ego's approach and stance toward inner life is formed in and through family relationships, it is changed through relationships. Our image of the ideal person is an image of the completely autonomous self. This is the heroic ideal, so compelling in our culture. The lone, self-sufficient hero is perceived as the apex of development, and the accompanying fantasy is that the highest form of self-development is completely "independent" development. This is a fantasy. It has been effectively critiqued as a fantasy by several schools of psychological thought (see Jean Baker Miller's *Toward a New Psychology of Women* as an example of the relational school of feminist psychology and Jessica Benjamin's *The Bonds of Love* as an example of the intersubjective school of psychoanalysis).[3] Internal relationships between aspects of the Self are formed and profoundly affected by external relationships. I believe it is virtually impossible to alter these internal relationships through autonomous action.

The most obvious and direct interpersonal relationship that will facilitate change in intrapsychic relationships is psychotherapy. Through modeling an interested, empathetic stance toward the client's process and toward the symbolic products of the unconscious and through reflecting on and challenging the hurtful aspects of the existing ego attitude the therapist can, over time, foster a shift in conscious attitude. Why must this happen over time? Because it is not solely, or perhaps even primarily, an intellectual process. Insight and cognitive understanding are extremely useful, but the primary tools of change are the therapist's reliable stance toward the client's Self and the therapist's patient willingness to address the ego's persistent attitude.

The ego's attitude is persistent because it was internalized in order to survive during childhood events that felt like life and death. In violent homes literal life and death might have been at stake. In other families love and acceptance, which are matters of survival to small children, may have been at stake. The therapist and client together produce an environment of acceptance and reflection and this can be internalized by the client, but it takes place through a necessary, spiraling, back-and-forth process. The form of this process can be seen in fairy tales when the protagonist must make several attempts at something (frequently three attempts) before reaching a turning point. Manypelts moves from downstairs to upstairs and back down repeatedly before she is recognized; the youth who set out to learn what fear was has multiple experiences of similar nature before his life changes. This is in some aspects a testing process, but it is also a form of learning that must go beyond intellectual learning. The shift in attitude toward the Self must sink in emotionally. This is analogous to developing "muscle memory" in sports training. This shift in attitude is the pragmatic support of separating from the old identity, the first stage of initiation, and it allows entrance into the second stage of liminal change.

Because the shadow tends to dominate a person's initial encounters with the unconscious and because the shadow is the part of the Self that is most challenging (often disgusting) to the ego's ideal image, it is potentially very disruptive to a newly developing ego attitude. This means that the newly emerging ego attitude is constantly being confronted with the most challenging material. An ally is needed to support the ego in its efforts until the emotional "muscle memory" develops. Although this period of time is a struggle it also scrvcs a useful purpose. The shadow is heavily freighted with personal memories, feelings, and experiences that are painful and unsettling. If a conscious *modus vivendi* can be made with this part of the Self, further exploration of the unconscious is less likely to be ambushed and derailed by unresolved pathology.

Relationships other than psychotherapy can also be useful in the process of changing the ego's attitude. For those whose issues include substance abuse or eating disorders, twelve-step programs can provide an environment and a structure that support serious change. Such programs have this effect only when they are rigorously followed, that is, when the participant has a sponsor and "works the steps." There is evidence that in recent years some twelve-step approaches have degenerated into forms of group victim identification. In attending a twelve-step group it is important to choose one that follows the AA "Big Book" format[4] and in which people have sponsors and work the steps.

Groups that form around political issues can also be a powerful influence on the ego's stance toward the Self, chiefly through the group's challenge to the culture's value system. Individuals may feel empowered by such a group to rethink their own social conditioning, to begin to develop independent values that might be more receptive to the shadowy parts of the Self. However, the political arena of "victim" causes is highly charged and overloaded with the rigid demands of political correctness. As a consequence people have profound, widely divergent experiences within this arena. Working in a wholesome and meaningful political movement can provide a powerful container for the resolution of victim identification. Unfortunately, some political groups support destructive and tenacious forms of victim identification while justifying self-righteous and abusive tactics. The biggest psychological danger in such groups lies in their replacing dominant cultural values with a rigid set of alternative values, a new persona identification that simply skews the communications of the Self through a different lens than the old persona. This is the pitfall of "identity politics." The Self is, in this instance, being codified in new terms but is still not allowed its unique destiny.

Spiritual groups share this danger with political groups; they may harbor as well the dangers springing from cult-like leadership. The philosophical and spiritual challenges presented by the existence of abuse, of evil, and of victims themselves make spiritual communities especially compelling, and if such communities are exploitive they are especially dangerous. However, if one is very careful in choosing a group and in assessing the effect that a given group appears to have on its members, then a spiritual practice may be very strengthening to the relationship with the Self. Meditation practices focusing on mindfulness seem to be especially helpful.

For those struggling with victim dynamics, relationships present opportunities for transformation or stagnation. Individual relationships are very influential whether they are friendships, work relationships, or romantic partnerships. The most evocative relationships in this regard are those involving authority and those involving romantic love. Freeing oneself from a victim identity requires one to assess the effects of these key relationships. On the most straightforward level this means making sure that one is not intimate with and vulnerable to people whose attitude toward oneself is disrespectful or undermining. That would of course support the victim persona. However, making such an assessment is not completely straightforward. The tone and attitude of a disrespectful inner voice may be projected outward, imagined as the secret commentary of others, or automatically read into their tone. An indication that this may be happening is the experience of "everyone sees me as X." In such generalizations the real individuality of the other is blurred. An additional complication in the process of assessing relationships lies in the fantasy, common among those who have been victimized in childhood, that they are the source of other people's bad behavior. This manifests in the conviction that although a friend, colleague, or partner may behave disrespectfully or problematically in most relationships, I should be able to find a way to act that will cause him or her to behave well, to be a different person with me. To guard against both of these distortions it is necessary to accept the limits on one's power and responsibility in relationships and to try to see the other as having a real, consistent personality of his or her own, not as having a personality that is contingent on or controlled by oneself.

This is a complex issue. Relationships are mutual productions, and at the same time people have their own consistent, predictable patterns of relating. In short, partners in relationship have their own characters and fates, both of which profoundly affect their behavior. Trying to find the balance between attending to one's own impact on an interaction without taking responsibility for the other person's behavior may require more than a cognitive analysis. The emotions and the body can communicate important perceptions about this balance. Taking on blame for someone else's behavior and demeanor produces certain trademark visceral reactions. Each person must develop awareness of her or his own particular responses, but in general, feelings of entrapment, helplessness, and intense personal failure, possibly accompanied by a somatic sense of being heavily burdened, are common indications of an imbalance in attribution of responsibility.

Wholesome relationships, which do not recapitulate abusive situations, can over time be internalized by the ego as an aspect of an internal reflective space. When trusted others notice one's responses in an accepting way and when they are not bowled over by those feelings, this can, over time, be taken in to build up the accepting attitude necessary for internal reflection. Mirroring, that is, accurate feedback from others, and recognition, that is, acknowledgment and appreciation of one's attributes, can be internalized as productive forms of self-reflection. The internal reflective space allows the opposites, which inevitably present themselves in internal and external life, to be tolerated. The temptation to handle such opposites in an absolutist, ideological way is rampant in the victim's experience and in the discourse on victims. The ability to reflect on opposites without falling into black-and-white thinking is fundamental to transforming victim identities. Otherwise the processes of demonization and beatification tend to contaminate attempts to understand and process experience. As a person develops more ability to reflect, more unconscious material is brought to consciousness, calling for certain ego skills and psychological capacities. These are also primarily developed through relationships.

Necessary Skills and Capacities

A person who is identified with a victim persona, whose experience of life is dominated, filtered, and skewed by that persona, is in the position of having to become prepared for a descent that is already in progress. Unlike an initiate in the ancient mystery religions who relied on lengthy teachings and ritual preparations as well as a guide in the process of descent, the victim's journey to the Underworld is in process while he or she struggles for the knowledge and skills necessary to foster a return. It is the ego, the conscious aspect of the Self, that must develop and maintain the skills that will enable it to work with entangled and highly charged symbolic material. In order to tolerate the liminal state necessary for dialogue with the unconscious, the ego must have certain abilities and properties.

Normal psychological development is a spiral of ego-Self separation and reunion.[5] The symbolic dialogue between ego and Self, taking place through the medium of the unconscious, is a dialogue of opposites. Symbolic material wells up from within to compensate and balance the ego's view and values. The ego normally and inevitably has a narrower view than the Self. When consciousness is made even narrower by identifying with a victim persona, dialogue with the Self is paradoxically more needed and less attainable. According to Jung, the ego needs two fundamental capacities in order to be an effective partner in symbolic dialogue. Those capacities are discrimination and containment. Taken together they build the ego container necessary for the liminal, mediating experiences vital to transformation.

Discrimination is fundamentally the ability to discern and delineate the components of inner life. Neutral, objective self-observation enables one to notice internal phenomena, to be interested in them, and to develop language or other forms of expression for them. Containment is the capacity to hold opposites, to tolerate and be interested in highly charged, emotional, and potentially disturbing communications from the unconscious once they are discriminated. The ego must be sturdy, flexible, and stable enough to explore conflicting parts of the Self without either leaping to action or becoming paralyzed. This is essentially the building of an internal reflective space, the internalizing of a container.

Some of the distortions of perception that are so noticeable in debates about victims result from the absence of the ego skills of discrimination and containment. The tendency to confuse a feeling of helplessness with true, circumstantial lack of power, for instance, reflects a lack of internal discrimination, an inability and/or unwillingness to distinguish inner and outer. A controversial illustration of this lies in the area of sexual harassment. A woman who is sexually propositioned by a man who has direct power over her job generally lacks the personal, individual power to rectify the problem. A very assertive woman who challenged her boss's behavior and whose boss was a fundamentally ethical, though obviously thoughtless, person, might be able to eliminate the problem alone, although she would be taking a big risk. However, given the probability that most people who proposition subordinates do not have especially well-developed ethics, most women will legitimately need external support and protection to rectify such a situation. If the importance of the abuse of power in these circumstances is denied or if external support in rectifying the situation is not forthcoming, those concerned receive a message that victimization is appropriate or perhaps is the victim's fault.

In contrast, when a woman experiences normal, subtle expressions of interest from a co-worker who actually does not have any power over her job and she feels helpless to draw a boundary with the co-worker, she is experiencing an inner feeling of helplessness rather than an externally enforced power differential. Often this point comes up only as a way of establishing blame for a difficult situation, that is, the woman's failure to draw a boundary, to act on her own behalf, will be used to invalidate her experience. Blame is not what makes the distinction between inner helplessness and outer helplessness important here. The distinction is psychologically important because, in a situation where the woman did have the power to make a personal boundary but would not or could not use that power, an external process, whether it is an in-house investigation, a union grievance, or a lawsuit, will not rectify the inner feeling of helplessness. (Remember that we are talking here about normal, subtle expressions of interest, not situations that involve violence or coercion.) The woman in that case remains dependent on others to maintain her personal boundaries. It may be that the experience of having an outside agency intervene between two adults of equal power will actually increase the feeling of inner helplessness, giving the indirect message, "Yes, you're right, you can't look after yourself." The ego must be able to discriminate inner from outer in order to choose an effective way of addressing the experience of helplessness. Using internal means to address an experience of powerlessness that is externally determined will result in paralysis and inappropriate self-blame. Addressing a reaction or feeling of inner powerlessness with external means will ultimately increase and support the feeling of powerlessness.

There are some who make the case that a woman or any member of a socially oppressed group always has less power than anyone from the socially dominant group. On the large scale this is probably true. On the small scale of interpersonal, one-on-one interactions, it is true only if there is coercion involved, such as an economic or physical threat, or if the psychological internalization of the social power differential has not been challenged by the individual involved. One must be able to notice, reflect on, and stand up to the internal assumptions, beliefs, and feelings that lead one to betray oneself, to forgo opportunities for empowerment. Many people seek to rely on ideological codification in an effort to clarify the more subtle experiences of helplessness. For instance, a female student of mine had been raised to believe that women were intellectually inferior. One way she tried to counteract this was to stop taking classes from male professors. Setting up rules like this in order to protect one's internal reactivity, the inner feeling of helplessness, creates many problems.

First and foremost, it doesn't work. As long as the shadow work is not done, reactivity will reappear, and it will be attached to a wider variety of experiences, forcing one's list of rules to grow ever longer. One's experience of life becomes more and more narrow. In addition, other people are rarely willing to be completely controlled by these rules, especially since the rules grow ever more demanding. Finally, if this process continues unabated, one begins to look ridiculous and becomes easy to invalidate. Meanwhile, the part of the Self that is lost in the Underworld and that is the source of the internal experience of powerlessness is being ignored by the ego. The internal victim is left unprepared for return while the individual is trying to create a world in which he or she will not have to be aware of or consciously deal with the descent that has already happened. Attempting to enforce rigid, codified rules for subtle human interactions is the result of an unwillingness to face the depths of one's own experience and history and the effect of that experience on the here and now.

Mary Gaitskill, in a beautifully balanced essay concerning her own experience of date rape and (in my terms) her subsequent identification with a victim persona, states:

> My critical rigidity followed from my inability to be responsible for my own feelings. In this context, being responsible would have meant that I let myself feel whatever discomfort, indignation or disgust I experienced without letting those feelings determine my entire reaction. . . . It would have meant dealing with my feelings and what had caused them rather than expecting the outside world to assuage them. I could have chosen not to see the world through the lens of my personal unhappiness and still had respect for my unhappiness.[6]

As she envisions holding onto the piercing subjective reality of her own pain while acknowledging the fact that things external to herself retain a meaning that is not determined solely by her reaction, Gaitskill is describing the nuts and bolts of the psychological containment of opposites.

Gaitskill also addresses the use of exaggerated, overblown, melodramatic language in victim discourse. Gaitskill uses the example of survivors of emotional abuse who call their childhood "a holocaust." To someone who survived the Nazi Holocaust or who lost loved ones in it this is, of course, an outrage. She puts her finger on one of its sources, saying, "To speak in exaggerated metaphors about psychic injury is not so much the act of a crybaby as it is a distorted attempt to explain one's own experience. . . . The distortion comes from a desperate desire to make one's experience have consequence in the eyes of others, and such desperation comes from a crushing doubt that one's own experience counts at all."[7] The desire that others should act in a way that relieves one of such a self-doubt is understandable but unreliable.

Grandiose analogies are a tragically useless strategy for recognition for two reasons. First, if others accept the overblown metaphor and respond in a comforting, reassuring way, the relief one experiences is only temporary. Reassurance does not rectify such a self-doubt; that must be done through work on the shadow problem, which in this case is being expressed in terms of severe self-doubt. As long as this work is not done the cycle of dramatically reciting the injury followed by temporary comfort will be repeated indefinitely. The second problem lies in the fact that most others will not accept an obviously overstated analogy and will instead perceive it as a conscious effort at manipulation. Since the perception is rarely accurate (I have seen conscious manipulation of this sort only in situations such as legal actions that involved material loss or gain) the person using the exaggerated language experiences even less recognition than before and her sense of self-doubt is increased rather than comforted. Despite these and other difficulties, the personal story, the particular tale of each person's story, needs to be told in some accepting context. The act of telling one's experiences in a coherent narrative and having those experiences recognized and acknowledged is intrinsically healing.

Recognition is more possible when words are found that convey the reality of a hurtful experience without inflating it. It may be that this is most important in the language one uses with oneself. If the internal dialogue is empathetic and heartfelt without being inflated then the dialogue one has with others will most likely follow in kind. Both processes of discrimination and a containment of opposites are involved. It is true that the emotional legacy of victimization is enormous in all victims. It is also true that there are gradations in external levels of injury. A destructive, even a dangerously violent family life is not equivalent to the attempted annihilation of an entire people, such as took place in the Holocaust. At the same time the depth of pain experienced by the child of such a family deserves a legitimate expression. Oscillating between the subjective validating of a feeling of annihilation and the objective reality of an act of annihilation, knowing both the difference and the similarity between the two, requires the ego to resist the temptation of choosing either the subjective or the objective. Tolerating truths that appear oppositional is not just an attempt to show respect to varieties of experience. It is also a process that can provide access to or make space for a transformative image emerging from the Self.

Transformative Images

As I look back on the tales in this book, I am left with certain vivid images, particularly of the resolutions of the stories: Persephone's reunion with Demeter, the sacred marriage of Beauty and the Beast, the Beast's transformation, the youth who set out to learn what fear was shuddering as little fish swim all over him, Manypelts's being recognized as she emerges from her hairy disguise, the wily sister in "Fitcher's Bird" transformed into a "wondrous bird," strolling down the road to freedom. These images hold the magical, transformative, yet deeply humorous and gritty quality of the archetypal aspect of the Self.

The Jungian view of human nature is a profoundly hopeful one, focusing on the unique destiny of each individual, relying on the immutable nature of the Self. The conscious manifestation of the Self may be constrained by circumstance, repressed or contorted by oppressive influences, but it is a resource that cannot be eliminated, and that is always available through the unconscious. In this respect the concept of the Self is a concept of radical freedom, the freedom offered by the validation of the inward journey of the psyche, the freedom of the symbolic reality of the personal myth. Symbolic reality does not compete with concrete reality, but it coexists with it, providing a freedom to change and grow that is unavailable in concrete life. It is important not to imply, as Freud seemed to or as many new age practitioners do, that symbolic reality supersedes concrete reality. The symbolic aspects of working through the legacy of abuse do not alter the necessity of dealing with abuse and oppression in the outer world. The spiritual and psychological work proposed in this book does not supplant or oppose the pragmatic work of fighting oppression, rather it complements it with internal development.

The crucial point is that the symbolic, mythic journey is always available as a path that maintains and develops the sense of self, a path that cannot be taken away by oppressive circumstance since its components and drive reside in the individual psyche. Grasping the value of this path requires a tolerance for ambiguity that is unusual in our dualistic culture. Bridging the concrete and the symbolic, as Persephone bridges the Upperworld and the Underworld, depends on one's willingness and ability to hold the tension of opposites. Tolerance of paradox is vital to understanding the dynamics of victimization. For both the victim and the abuser, tolerating the coexistence of equal opposites is crucial to internally resolving the disfiguring and contradictory effects of victimization.

As in genuine, open dialogue between disagreeing individuals, rigid and extreme elements of the psyche can be mediated by the dialectical effect of their opposites. All points of view are partial and will be modified in the course of both internal and external dialogue.[8] Marie-Louise von Franz gives us a description of this dialogue process as she uses it in her method of myth interpretation:

> Psychological interpretation is our way of telling stories. . . . We know quite well that this [constitutes] our myth. . . . Therefore we should never present our interpretation with the undertone of "this is it.". . . The criterion is: Is it satisfactory and does it click with me and other people? And do my own dreams agree?[9]

She also states that she must know limits of her own consciousness in the process of constructing the interpretive story and that she expects others to go beyond those limits, superseding her understanding.

In a similar way, those who are struggling with a victim identity must attend to the limits of their own consciousness, exposing those limits to the continuously modifying effects of dialogue: dialogue with motifs that well up from within the unconscious (do one's dreams agree?) and with the subjective truth of other people's stories. This dialectic is particularly suited to the postmodern condition, in which absolute meanings are no longer possible. It is, however, a difficult and anxiety-provoking stance to maintain. The impermanence of our conceptual constructs, the shifting of meanings from story to story that von Franz so calmly describes, can be, *in vivo,* a deeply confusing experience for the ego. Ideology and reification are both tempting solutions to the confusion. The temptation to reify a useful experience or narrative image gives the ego an opportunity to identify with a habitual worldview, to settle back into a comfortable illusion of control. The dialectic of opposites, however, allows habitual consciousness to be influenced, balanced, and expanded by the rediscovery of lost truths, truths that evolve in process, in ongoing shared narrative.

The healthy ego's task is to tolerate the tension of being conscious of truths that seem contradictory. This is a liminal experience, a state of ambiguous possibility that, because the mind is not busily pursuing and nailing down a position or stuck in a seemingly unresolvable debate of opposing pros and cons, creates room for the emergence of a mediating symbol. The symbol presents not a solution for the contradiction but fresh terms for choice. At a time in my life when I was convinced that I had to stay committed to an extremely hectic schedule I also had many somatic and emotional experiences that indicated a desire to stop working altogether. Bringing this conflict to awareness and living with it consciously for a while produced a number of dream images that led me to see the conflict in terms of how I was working rather than how much I was working. Obviously someone outside the conflict, that is, someone without strong emotional involvement with either side of the internal debate, might be able to think of a similar response to the impasse. However, such a solution offered from outside the experience of the conflict often prompts a response along the lines of "Yes, that makes sense but. . . ." It is important for the mediating experience to develop within the person who suffers the conflict of the opposites. Solutions from without, however logical and appealing, often have a pasted-on quality and the more intense the emotional charge of the impasse, the less staying power such a solution will have. The impasse suffered by the victim-identified is highly charged, and having felt betrayed by trusted individuals and by society, their openness to an external solution is even lower than normal. A shift that comes from within is even more important.

Making internal room for images, space in which mediating symbols can develop, is for most people a conscious, directed task. The time and attention required to notice, record, and attend to a dream image is not easily reserved. Time spent on the inner life of the Self is rarely seen as important. It is often considered trivial—at best a hobby, at worst a narcissistic activity. However, it is a basic step in developing the internal container. Both clients and students have complained to me that symbolic images do not come to them. When I have explored this with them I have almost always found that images do come to them, but they dismiss the images in some way as unworthy of attention. This is, once again, a problem of the ego's attitude, reflecting sometimes a fear of the content of the images or a desire for more exciting images. The individual must be willing to discover the archetypal narrative that is unfolding in his or her life and to forgo the temptation of trying to choose more appealing symbols than the ones that spontaneously emerge. Using myth and fairy tale to uncover the depth in one's own story is more important than choosing the "correct" myth or tale to relate to or use as some sort of template. The stories used in this book give us many marvelous hints about healing: Demeter's barley-water and the laughter that connects her larger-than-life grief to the everyday world; Beauty's mirror that shows the suffering shadow-Beast; the youth's confrontation with internalized contempt in the form of a nasty old man whose beard is trapped in a split anvil; Manypelts's hearty soup, made in captivity and still holding the Cracker Jack surprise that leads to recognition; the wily sister's skull dressed as a bride, her bold depiction of the evil truth. These hints can guide us as we discover and weave together the personal and transpersonal aspects of our own myth.

Following images that spontaneously emerge can lead to delineating a personal myth, which provides structure for the identity that develops in the third stage of initiation. Dream images in particular should be explored from both personal and transpersonal perspectives, since they have roots in both parts of the unconscious. Associations to the dream image from personal life and history can lead to a deeper understanding of oneself and one's problems. Associations, even to the same image, from myth and folklore can provide hints about the transpersonal aspect of the psyche.

For instance, while writing this book I dreamed that I had been cast in a play with a medieval theme. I seemed to be in charge of a sword, of which I could not keep track. I told the director of the play that I had been miscast. My personal associations to these images led me to explore my fears about writing this book. The sword made me think of the "cutting through" aspects of analysis and thought, and my fear in the dream that I was not the best keeper of such a tool helped me to notice some buried concerns I had about my analyses of the stories in this volume. I needed to revisit some experiences of my adolescence, which were the source of one aspect of this anxiety. I also needed to rely more on my editor's advice, since some of my fears were entirely justified. This was practical help inspired by mulling over the dream, but more was offered by the symbols involved.

In order to amplify the archetypal level of the dream images I began to browse through medieval stories looking for women with swords, and this, of course, led rather quickly to the Lady of the Lake in the King Arthur legend. When I reread Arthur's first encounter with the Lady of the Lake, in which she gives him his sword, I felt intrigued, moved on the gut level. This feeling-level response is, for me, key to the process of archetypal amplification. The archetypal level of a symbol carries a strong emotional charge, for it partakes of the archetype's numinous aura. A strong, gut-level, felt response is, I believe, a more reliable guide than a cognitive interpretation because the transpersonal aspect of the unconscious, the mythic level, cannot be expressed in purely intellectual terms. When exploring the archetypal aspect of a dream image it is not necessary or even desirable to prove that a given association is the "correct" one. It is necessary that the association feel meaningful and that it lead somewhere. In this case it led me to explore the Celtic underpinnings of the image of the Lady of the Lake, an exploration that yielded more images and a fuller story than the Lady is accorded in Arthur's myth. These stories have come to inform and inspire the creative part of my life. Certainly if I had decided to go looking for a myth to relate to I might have happened upon the same material, but my experience of its meaningfulness would have been quite different, more theoretical. My dream-world connection to the mythic images helps me feel their numinous charge rather than simply be interested in them; it helps me experience my life's vital connection to levels beyond the everyday. And such exploration of the archetypal level of the psyche typically brings with it more dreams, further information about the personal myth.

In this example I hope to convey the multivalent, liminal nature of symbolic images and the way in which one can use multiple ways of knowing—cognitive, emotional, somatic, imaginal—to explore the potential inherent in such images. It is this potential that opens the transformative resources of the psyche, resources desperately needed by anyone who is identified with a victim persona. If, as Jung believed, the psyche is a "door that opens upon the human world from a world beyond, allowing unknown and mysterious powers to act upon man and carry him on the wings of the night to a more than personal destiny,"[10] then the psyche can provide the impetus to transcend destructive and oppressive elements of that personal destiny.

The victim who is trapped in everyday constraints on the self can transcend preoccupation with those constraints and tap into the expanded viewpoint of the Self, which includes both the everyday and the mythic, the personal and the transpersonal. That expanded view is healing and freeing in and of itself. It also provides energy and insight which can flow back into the everyday situation, helping the ego to deal with difficult circumstances.

CHAPTER EIGHT

PERSEPHONE ON OPRAH

The Cultural Significance of the Victim's Descent

The drama of the victim is all around us in contemporary America. On any randomly chosen afternoon talk show one is likely to hear a tale of abuse. Suffering, redemption, and revenge, the basic plot points of the victim story, have always been staples of great literature and theater, but the contemporary victim's tale is distinguished by its emphasis on blame and entitlement. The need to establish blame for suffering has become so pervasive that even natural disasters, the well-known "acts of God" such as floods or earthquakes, inspire blaming commentary like, "Why should the rest of us help people who are foolish enough to live in such dangerous places?" Talk shows often feature competing victims, people who are in conflict with each other and who present their cases to the audience for adjudication. The verdict consists of a decision concerning who has really been injured, who is the more righteous victim. People are held responsible for things they cannot control and are relieved of responsibility for their own acts. Who is entitled to sympathy, help, understanding, respect? Who deserves approbation and who deserves scorn? Who is to blame? These are the compelling questions, so compelling that people are more than willing to expose themselves to an audience of strangers in a television studio, an audience that then supports or condemns them, tells them if they are entitled to revenge, comfort, or blame.

These abuse tales are told and retold, varying in detail but similar in basic form. As evidenced by television ratings (and by other measures such as best-selling confessional memoirs of abuse), the journey of the victim fascinates us. The tellers of victim tales constitute a loosely connected, informal movement with both political and spiritual implications. Often a particular social or political group identity is crucial to the victim's story and a claim for uniqueness of suffering is made (for example, racism causes more pain than sexism), yet plots and character types are fairly consistent in stories from group to group. I believe that the ubiquitousness of the story and the furious conflict it arouses mean that the victim's descent to the Underworld is a narrative with mythic significance for contemporary American culture. The prominence of the story itself and the potency of the story's form—its ability to invoke strong feelings of all kinds from people of almost any political orientation—indicates its archetypal force. In such a heated cultural context the individual will find it hard to work through issues on a solely personal level. Mythic ideas are being worked out by individuals in their efforts to understand their own journeys, but on a large scale something about the collective myth of American culture is being worked out. The victim's descent to the Underworld and the victim's return or failure to return have a hold on collective consciousness because they point toward something that is missing from collective consciousness.

An Underworld journey typically leads to rectifying an imbalance. In a popular story of the Pacific Northwest Raven the trickster hero goes on an Underworld journey to the dark, forbidding lodge of a chief who keeps the sun and moon hidden away from humankind. The lodge and its denizens would seem familiar to us after reading of the various haunted castles and enchanted palaces in our fairy tales. Raven goes through many transformations, including one that brings him into human form, and finally he returns from the dark lodge with the gift of light and a restoration of the cycle of dark and light. As Joseph Campbell says, "You go into a depth. . . . There you come to what was missing in your consciousness in the world you formerly inhabited."[1] Raven's descent and return provide a missing piece in the story of how the cosmos works, about what it takes to journey in the dark to a frightening place that hides special resources; it conveys something about the place of human consciousness in relation to the forces of nature, about the proper relationship between the dark and the light.

A culture's collective picture of the cosmos and of the human's place in it, the cultural worldview, is established and maintained by the culture's mythic system, a group of stories that the majority of people accept as true. This is as true for a culture like ours, which sees itself as "scientific" in outlook, as it is for a culture holding what we would call a more mythic view. Historically, narratives of descent have served a distinct purpose in the development of mythic systems. In the resolution of the descent narrative a different relationship between Upperworld and Underworld is established, a boon or insight is brought into the conscious life of the group. The told and retold tale of the descent and return, when it becomes part of the group of accepted stories, affects the collective world view by incorporating this new insight.

The contemporary victim's narrative of descent into

abuse and attempted redemption or return is a part of this tradition. The highly charged debate on the proper forms of victim redemption is a conflict about the nature of the new insight that must be incorporated into our worldview. In other words, the victim has gone down into the depths, and now she has returned to tell the tale, to convey what she has found, and to describe the boon or insight that was missing from collective consciousness. There follows in the social discourse a battle concerning the proper interpretation of her tale, a conflict about the appropriate relationship between the Upperworld and the Underworld. Does her Underworld journey tell us that we must do more for her or that she must do more for herself? Who is to blame? Is she a hero or a pariah? And what do the answers to these questions mean about human nature, about the way the world works, about the human being's proper place in relationship to the forces of nature? The victim's story of descent and return is an archetypal narrative that has emerged in our culture at this time for a collective, compensatory purpose. The current dominance of this particular story in popular culture indicates a broadly based, unconscious, symbolic attempt to balance the Western world's picture of the way things work, the collectively held image of life's structure.

In classical Greece this cultural balance was provided by the myth and ritual of Persephone's Underworld journey. The Greek worldview forms one of the bases of the Western worldview, and many of the underpinnings of that ancient vision are still embedded in our assumptions about the way everything, including human nature, works. Looking at the effect of Persephone's descent and return on the Greek image of the world and the human being's place in that world will help us to understand our own obsession with the victim's descent.[2]

What Did Persephone Bring Back?

Earlier I spoke of Persephone's descent as the archetypal victim's journey. What does her story tell us about the collective meaning of the victim's narrative, as it was experienced at the dawn of Western culture? In the rape of Persephone, the journeyer does not go by choice into the Underworld but is coerced into descent. The chthonic realm, the Underworld, is split off from the Upperworld almost completely, with no access other than death. It is a vague place, and the initiatory processes of entering the nether realm are not described in the story. The rites of passage that might enable one to negotiate a descent without being destroyed are unknown and unpictured to the living. This lack of connection between Upperworld and Underworld, life and death, reflects the original patriarchal Greek view of the cosmos.[3]

In Hesiod's *Theogony,* a seventh-century B.C.E. poem that delineates Greek patriarchal cosmology, Zeus establishes universal order.[4] His cosmic order depends on the strict separation of spheres of influence among the Gods and a radical separation of Gods and humans. Hades's sphere of influence, the Underworld, is cut off from other realms, and rebirth from the Underworld becomes a violation of cosmological order. The cycle of destruction and regeneration, descent and return, is interrupted, or, more accurately, images and narratives that allow a conscious relationship to that cycle are not available in Zeus's cosmos.

Hades is faceless, and his main attribute is his helmet of

invisibility. He generally functions as a *deus ex machina* in powerful myths that say little about him or his qualities. The myth of Persephone's rape says nothing about Hades's apparently sudden desire for a wife. He is given no motive for raping Persephone, as opposed to courting her or perhaps choosing a willing wife. Of all the Greek Gods, who are notorious for their detailed personalities and multiple exploits, Hades is close to unknowable. He is also unknowing. Hades is portrayed as having no direct knowledge of the Upperworld. He can grasp only what the shades of the dead may relate to him, if he cares to ask. One meaning of his name is "sightless"[5] and he seems to be fundamentally uninterested in anything outside his confined realm. When Hades puts in an appearance in someone else's story, he is often complaining to his younger brother Zeus about some violation of privilege or protocol. Particularly in stories involving the raising of the dead, he complains of the loss of his property, the ghosts. This is a striking indication of the way in which the concept of rebirth after destruction became unnatural in Greek cosmology and living human beings had no link with the Underworld, no way of preparing for or consciously negotiating a descent or envisioning a return. The universe was split in two, the realm of light and growth having no natural connection to the realm of dark and decay.

Greek cosmology before Persephone's descent depicts a dualistic universe in which such opposites as order and chaos, male and female, transcendence and immanence, human and divine, upper and lower are delineated and separated, ordered and controlled. This dualism has strong associations with a split in gender imagery. The feminization of descent is part of a pattern of gender associations. The Greeks began to link men to culture and women to nature, effecting a strict and severe separation of male and female spheres in everyday life and in divine cosmology. The separation was accompanied by a clear hierarchy in which the values of transcendence, control, progress, power, and mind (nous), identified as superior, were linked with masculinity. Chthonic aspects of life and the values of immanence, emotion, and vulnerability were devalued and linked with the feminine. This dualistic worldview was to become dominant in Western culture, mirroring the split between Upperworld and Underworld. With male divine figures firmly restricted to their specified, separate kingdoms, it is left to a female figure to bridge the resulting divisions and to try, through her Underworld journey, to reconnect the split aspects of experience.

Persephone eventually provides a way to relate Upperworld to Underworld. She evolves from a victimized, helpless Kore (a maiden without a name) into a Goddess who traverses the two worlds; her suffering and helplessness are transformed through her individuation. As the connector of divided worlds through her eternal cycle of descent and return, she embodies the archetypal process of bridging the opposites, a process that Jung identifies as fundamental to the realization of the Self. This is the modification of the binary cosmos, the transcending of Zeus's original strict separation of realms of experience. The liminal mediation of this split is the missing aspect of consciousness that Persephone finds in the depths of her journey and embodies in her return.

In the late nineteenth century, anthropologist James

Fraser, in *The Golden Bough,* interpreted cycles of descent and return in myth as mere metaphors for the cycle of the seasons.[6] His reductionistic view seems to appeal to our materialistic culture. Consequently, the modern reader expects Persephone's descent to coincide with the beginning of winter and her return to be synonymous in time with the spring equinox. In fact, her return well precedes the equinox in the earliest versions of the story, and we are not told when she descends again to Hades. Additionally, in later myths like that of Orpheus or the many others who undertake a journey to the Land of the Dead, Persephone is always in her nether kingdom, no matter what the season in the Upperworld.[7] And in stories involving Demeter, Persephone is always with her in the Upperworld. As a simple metaphor for seasonal change Persephone is not very efficient. She is in fact paradoxical, as befits an embodiment of opposites.

When commentary has gone beyond Fraser's simplistic view, it has focused on the myth as social commentary on classical Greek family structure. Persephone is ecstatically reunited with a powerful mother and then oscillates between matriarchal and patriarchal realms. Greek daughters and sons were removed from their mother's embrace at very young ages, never to return. Young adolescent girls were given to a form of marriage that made them the sequestered property of the husband's family, and the boys were removed almost completely to a man's world of competition and striving by age five or six. Socially, the mother was cut off from the child and the child's pragmatic fate was controlled by an oppressive family structure. In everyday life there was no return to the world of the mother.

Is the historical devotion of the Greeks to the myth of Persephone and the associated mystery rites basically a form of compensation? A fantasy of regression to the maternal refuge, a fantasy unconsciously designed to soothe the wounds of harsh child-rearing practices? This is another reductionistic view, often found in psychoanalytic commentary, and it ignores a more profound truth. The imagery, narrative, and rites concerning Persephone's loss of innocence, descent, and return provide a form and a process for psychological survival. Myth and ritual are gateways to emotional, psychological, and spiritual resources for people in life situations that could otherwise destroy the sense of Self. The individual who is bound by severe and possibly abusive social constraints can experience the passion of the story as a union of opposites and as a pattern for internal rebirth that cannot be controlled by external circumstances.

Through her rape, abduction, suffering, and transformation into a Queen of the Underworld who retains her link to the Upperworld, Persephone becomes the liminal figure that is missing in Zeus's patriarchal ordering of the cosmos. She causes Demeter to reassert the power of the Earth Mother and she connects Hades to the Upperworld. She is concerned with the breaking down of the divisions Zeus has so carefully delineated.[8] "Persephone opens a new path to the world below through her annual descent and ascent. Mortals now have an ear in the Underworld and the universe has a link between heaven, earth and the world below."[9] Persephone is a symbol of a cosmic process of connection, not a metaphor for a concrete process. Through Demeter's intervention she reembodies the cosmic force of death and regeneration, a force that defies and overwhelms the patriarchal attempt to order and control nature. Persephone provides the flowing connection, the liminal potential for transformation missing from Zeus's original binary picture of the cosmos. Through her rites, the Eleusinian Mysteries, she also provides human beings with a way to reconnect the split worlds. The balancing story was enacted through a balancing ritual experience. This is also what Persephone brought back from the Underworld.[10]

In the Eleusinian Mysteries, the ancient ritual enactment of the myth of Persephone's descent and return, the *mystae* (the initiates) embraced this reconnection of the split worlds. The initiates in the mysteries "lived the miracle of intimacy with the goddesses, experienced their presence, were received into the sphere of their acts and suffering, into the reality of their sublime being. This was no mere looking on but a transformation of being."[11] This is an aspect of what anthropologists call *participation mystique,* which is a feeling of oneness that can come about in rituals overcoming the separation between subject and object. Persephone's liminal reconnecting of the split worlds is reflected in the intimate personal experience of the *mystae* during the ritual. The mystery rites gave initiates the *experience* of descent, suffering, and return in a safe, spiritual container. Individual human beings were connected to both Upperworld and Underworld; the mundane, everyday experience of loss was connected to the divine losses and transformations of the Goddesses, giving loss and suffering a sacred, bearable meaning. With that experience, the initiates at Eleusis spiritually resolved, through Persephone's story, the life problem presented to them by their patriarchal culture's dualistic, schismatic, schematic worldview.

Persephone's "divine ambivalence,"[12] as anthropologist Marija Gimbutas calls it, balances the stultifying exactness of masculinized cosmology and epistemology, an exactness that cannot address the mystery of eternal suffering and redemption, destruction and rebirth—the cyclic mystery that cannot be avoided but must somehow be embraced.

Contemporary Stories of Descent

It is precisely that acceptance of the cycle of destruction and rebirth that is conspicuously missing from present-day victim narratives. Returning to the notorious talk show display of victims' suffering, we can speculate that the format of confession, audience response, comfort, advice and in the case of at least one show, on-the-air revenge[13] is an unconscious attempt to create the kind of ritual experience of meaning and resolution for the victim's story that was provided by the Eleusinian Mysteries. The age-old mythic form of the descent and return is activated. But in our contemporary narratives the journey is not resolved, the balancing of collective consciousness usually brought about by the Underworld journey has not been forthcoming. What stands in the way of this resolution? The chief obstacle is the way in which contemporary stories of the Underworld journey portray descent as unnatural. Suffering, loss, vulnerability, and pain are spoken of as deeply disruptive to "normalcy." I am not implying that abuse and oppression should be accepted or condoned as normal. However, unfairness and suffering are unavoidable aspects of being human; one could say they are a normal aspect of being incarnate. To avoid becoming stuck in a repetitive, unresolved cycle of victim stories, individuals and cultures must come to a somewhat paradoxical view of suffering. That view is perhaps put best in the AA prayer, which asks for the strength to change what can be changed, the serenity to accept what can't be changed, and the wisdom to know the difference.

Injustices that are occurring now can *sometimes* be rectified now, and injustices which occurred in the past and involved material injury can be partially rectified through money or services. However, injustices that occurred in the past and that have left a psychological, emotional, and/or spiritual legacy can be addressed only by those experiencing the effects: the victims. If we think back to Gaitskill's example of date rape from the earlier discussion, we can delineate these different levels of possible response. Gaitskill, as a victim of date rape, could, if she chose and if the statute of limitations had not run out, institute either criminal or civil proceedings against the man involved (note: she does not report doing this). This might dissuade him from repeating the offense. It might provide Gaitskill with monetary resources for reparative therapy, and it might give her a sense of validation about her injury. These are all legitimate goals. Of course she could lose a legal proceeding and receive none of these possible benefits. In either case, once these pragmatic and concrete courses of action were exhausted, Gaitskill would still have to internally work through the effect of the experience on herself, philosophically coming to terms with the meaning of such experiences and deciding how to protect herself from any future possible incidents (she seems to have done all three in her essay).

The ancient mystery cults assumed that no one ascends from the Underworld unmarked. This is manifestly true, yet in contemporary American culture people seem to expect to be unmarked by their own histories. It seems possible that this attitude is historically related to our status as a nation in which the majority are immigrants or descendants of immigrants—people who literally have left personal history behind them. Among American people there seems to be little preparation for or expectation of suffering and considerable expectation of some type of invulnerability. More than a goal or fantasy, this expectation, an aspect of the heroic ideal, sometimes assumes the proportions of a moral imperative, as if it were somehow unrighteous to be marked by an experience of descent, an experience of victimization. Curiously, those who become obsessed with the marks of their victim experiences seem to be pursuing the same fantasy. The victim-identified appear to be seeking a remodeling of the past—seeking to be innocent and unmarked again through finding someone to blame, a person or group who can then be forced to provide rectification. In general, there is enormous confusion about the difference between injuries that are preventable or rectifiable and those that are inevitable—the losses that are a part of the human condition and must be dealt with spiritually, emotionally, and psychologically rather than concretely.

In our collective consciousness the Underworld and all it connotes of the inevitability of human vulnerability and loss has become so separate from the Upperworld of progress and heroic endeavor that it has lost its place as a real, inevitable part of the universe. Elaine Pagels attributes this to the dominance in the modern West of Augustine's dogma, originally adopted by the Roman Empire as orthodoxy in the fifth century: "Augustine assures the sufferer that pain is unnatural, death an enemy, [they are] alien intruders upon normal human existence." For Augustine, the Upperworld of the righteous and heroic (the true Christian) has no normal or natural involvement with the Underworld of the sufferer, the victim (the sinner). Pagels believes that the long-term hegemony of the Augustine worldview has caused it to become embedded as an assumption dominating the collective Western worldview, regardless of the specific, present-day religious beliefs or nonbeliefs of particular individuals or countries.[14]

I am not a religious scholar like Pagels, and so I cannot fully assess her analysis of the historical source of this worldview, but her description of it fits my own perception. Certainly the stories dominating the airwaves seem to partake of the assumption that "pain is unnatural, death an enemy, alien intruders upon normal human existence." The picture of existence springing from this premise encourages people either to blame the sufferer—suffering is unnatural and so the sufferer is unnatural, that is, shameful—or to perceive the suffering as an outrageous imposition, an alien experience that can never be assimilated but must somehow be eliminated, perhaps through denial, revenge, or grandiose reparation. Blame and entitlement, the emotional foundations for denial and revenge, emerge therefore as constant themes. We are entitled to perfect happiness and security. If we don't have it someone must be responsible, and if they are brought to justice that must somehow rectify our deprivation.

In a way Zeus's original cosmological picture, unmodified by Persephone's transformation of it, persists in modern Western culture. Upperworld and Underworld are split off from one another. All perceived opposites are strictly separated in a dualistic world picture. As a consequence our world picture has virtually no image or concept of loss and destruction as inevitable, sometimes necessary, or even potentially fruitful. Dominant Western consciousness is in love with progress. Progress is variously seen as inevitable, unstoppable, and ordained. Progress may be threatened in some instances, but it is always treated as a prime virtue, obtainable through hard work and striving. The Western deification of progress and perfect order leaves little room for the messy reality of natural cycles of creation and destruction, the cycle of descent and return as it manifests in nature at large or in human nature. Death, loss, and decay are split off from and inimical to that which is deemed good and wholesome. This caused and causes the human experiences of vulnerability, helplessness, and disintegration, those aspects of being human that make one susceptible to death and loss, to be split off as well. These experiences, the fundamental experiences of victimization, are denied value; they become unknown, demonized, and associated with the feminine. The associated potential for regeneration and transformation also becomes split off and is unacknowledged.[15]

The demonization of cyclical processes discounts the inevitability of cycles of disintegration and the occasional necessity of disaster. The efficient prevention of forest fires in the giant sequoia groves of Yosemite has also prevented the trees from reproducing. Apparently the sequoias need the periodic destruction of the lightning fires in order to begin anew. This could serve as a metaphor for the modern psychological situation in which necessary experiences of disintegrative vulnerability are repressed and regeneration is stymied. Dan, a client I mentioned briefly earlier, experienced a number of feelings about his work that seemed to indicate he simply did not enjoy the tasks his profession demanded of him. Dan was fortunate in the sense that he had the financial resources to support a career change. Despite this he found it tremendously difficult to even contemplate changing to a more satisfying job. The main obstacle seemed to be that Dan firmly believed that it was intrinsically dangerous to pay attention to any reaction or feeling that did not directly support a straight line of progress. The intense, vulnerable feelings he experienced about his work, although disturbing and disruptive, were the heralds of a potentially positive change, but they were automatically perceived as invalid because they did not immediately further material, linear progress.

Our addiction to progress leaves us with a cultural shadow problem. Normal vulnerability is demonized, and the potential for change and rebirth that is seeded within vulnerability is lost. On a large scale, the American belief that it is possible to live without normal loss and with constant growth prevents us from recognizing that growth requires internal space cleared by loss. The hero persona, which supports this grandiose fantasy, leads us to treat loss and renewal as mutually exclusive opposites rather than as linked experiences. The supposedly perfect autonomy of the hero means that we regard the Underworld of vulnerability as the domain of the victim, entirely separate from the hero's Upperworld. The insight and gift that Persephone brought back from the Underworld at the beginning of Western culture is seemingly lost. The liminal, divine ambivalence of Persephone, the powerful "ambiguous space"[16] she embodies, is the great cultural shadow of the West, the psychological experiences and capacities that are not valued or developed in our society.

It was Jung's opinion that the ego-dominated, hyper-rational, materialist stance of the Western psyche gives rise to a loss of meaning in the experience of life. The heroic ideal alienates people from meanings that are felt rather than intellectually constructed; it invalidates meaningful experiences that are rooted and experienced in emotion, symbol, somatic experience, or spiritual life. Emphasis on personal autonomy, control, and individualism as psychological norms causes the individual to be isolated, alienated from others and from the natural world. Nature, whether experienced in the earth or in the body, cannot be controlled by individual willpower. The individual human being is vulnerable to nature; we are small in its scheme. The heroic ideal will not acknowledge this fact, promoting instead a grandiose image of the human being in relationship to nature. This is one of the reasons that "people socialized in the modern worldview emerge as strangers in the cosmos."[17] Alienation from meaning would seem to be directly related to dualism as it manifests in a variety of cultural splits. The separation of the human individual from nature at large is one manifestation of the Upperworld/Underworld split that separates the progress-oriented hero who quests for control from the victim who is caught in nature's cyclical processes.

Commentary on the prevalence of the victim's story often focuses on the irrationality of the victim's claims of injury and her requests for rectification (see Wendy

Kaminer's *It's all the Rage,* for example)[18] but little interest is shown in possible reasons for the prevalence of these irrational expressions. The appeal of the irrational in this context is usually understood as defensive pathology, a way of avoiding personal responsibility and effort. It may be instead that when people use irrational terms to grapple with victimization, they are in fact groping for a way to express and come to terms with something truly mysterious, something operating on a larger scale than personal injury and personal reparation, something that cannot completely be accounted for through rational analysis.[19] As Jung says, "A myth is being played out in the unconscious, a myth that extends over centuries, a stream of archetypal ideas that goes on . . . through individuals . . . like a continuous stream. . . . It comes to light in spiritual and political movements."[20] An ancient myth concerning the relationship between the individual human being and the cyclical forces of nature is being played out on our cultural stage, but without resolution.

Conclusion

In contemporary America the victim is unprepared for descent. The culture provides no preparation or framework for something that is seen as unnatural, that should not happen. Social conditioning is oriented toward preventing descent, toward being heroic, perfect, careful, and sinless enough to avoid all suffering. No one chooses to become vulnerable and so, when the time comes in which vulnerability is inevitable, the sufferer has no practice in dealing with it, no useful way to make the experience meaningful. In ancient descent stories the protagonist completes an initiation and returns from the Underworld with an insight, ritual, or gift for the culture. The contemporary victim's initiatory experience is consistently being short-circuited by the way in which blame and entitlement dominate all efforts to make meaning out of the Underworld journey. "We remain captive to a binary discourse of accusation and counter-accusation, grievance and counter-grievance, victims and victimizers."[21] The binary discourse is a direct descendant of the binary worldview, which leaves us in a descent with no plan for return.

Because the processes of return and transformation include aspects of the psyche and of experience that are mysterious and that resist rational explanation, our culture has no conscious way of facilitating those processes. Without a bridging of this split worldview, a balancing modification and shift in consciousness like the one provided by the Persephone myth in Greek cosmology, the descent must be made again and again, told again and again. A battle of worldviews is fought around the victim's story, a battle in which opposing camps try to persuade and pressure each other to accept a particular resolution to the narrative. However, only a medial bridging of our binary worldview will resolve the Underworld journey.

Persephone's mediation of the split between Underworld and Upperworld is still accessible to us. "The tradition of the mysteries was driven into the unconscious by the dominant forces of Western culture, but it carries with it values missing from Western consciousness which must be reintegrated if Western civilization is to achieve wholeness. The mystery religions have important insights into the nature of the soul, initiation and rebirth, and the relationship between the human being and the cosmos."[22] If the mystery of the cyclical connection between disintegration and regeneration has a conscious place in the collective worldview, it will no longer be necessary for particular individuals or groups to carry the burden of connecting Underworld to Upperworld through embodying victim personae. When the heroic ideal is balanced by the insights available through conscious descent, disenfranchised social groups will no longer have to carry the brunt of victimizing circumstances and the burden of descent imagery in our collective mythos. When Western society is able to distinguish between unnecessary suffering caused by the abuse of power and the inevitable losses caused by normal human vulnerability, then the meaning of the victim's Underworld journey will be resolved. The story of the victim's descent will, at that point, cease to dominate our popular culture.

In his book, *Mississippi*, Anthony Walton recounts a journey in which he confronts his family's history. After taking in the depth of oppression, rage, and dehumanization suffered by his parents and grandparents as sharecroppers in the rural South, Walton comes to the necessary resolution:

> We Americans love to think ourselves innocent of the tragedies—personal and public—that the past and our compulsions have visited upon us, all of us. Most of all, we want to be innocent of how much the ghosts and bones of our beautiful landscape have shaped and twisted virtually everything that has happened here; and we want to remain ignorant of how costly our innocence is to our government, our communities and our hearts. . . . it is my great lesson to

> have learned to stop trying to evade and forget what I have seen and heard and understood and now must know, but rather to embrace the ghosts and cradle the bones and call them my own.[23]

To place Walton's experience into the framework of a descent story, he has descended into the Underworld of victimization and he has brought back the aspect of consciousness which was missing in the Upperworld of everyday life. By embracing the ghosts and cradling the bones within ourselves and within our collective history we may finally experience the mediation promised by Persephone's eternal return.

CHAPTER NOTES

CHAPTER ONE

1. See Chapter Two. Persephone was a goddess of the Underworld; she was the only child of Zeus and Demeter. Carried off by Hades to the Underworld her archetypal journey back and forth from the Underworld to the Upperworld typifies a universal journey that illustrates a deeper psychological principle of death and rebirth that we will explore throughout this book. The myth of Persephone is adapted from Robert Graves, *The Greek Myths* (Hamondsworth, England: Penguin, 1974). For more information on this myth see also Edward Tripp, *Crowell's Handbook of Classical Mythology: An Alphabetical Guide to the Myths of Greece and Rome, Real and Legendary, including Place Names and Literary Sources* (New York: Thomas Y. Crowell Company, 1970), p.463–4.

The fairy tales, The Youth Who Set Out to Learn What Fear Was in Chapter Four, Manypelts in Chapter Five, and Fitcher's Bird in Chapter Six are adapted from *The Complete Grimms' Fairytales* (New York: Pantheon, 1944, 1972), p.29–39, p.326–331, p.216–219.

2. Judith Herman, *Trauma and Recovery* (New York: Basic Books, 1992), p.7–31.

3. C.J. Jung, *Collected Works*, VII (1966), *Two Essays on Analytical Psychology*, p.123–241. The publication of the first complete edition, in English, of the works of Carl Gustav Jung was undertaken by Routledge and Kegan Paul, Ltd., in England and by the Bollingen Foundation in the United States. The American edition is number XX in the Bollingen Series, which since 1967 has been published by Princeton University Press. Coincidentally the complete series contains twenty volumes including a general index and a bibliographic volume. Throughout the notes of this text CW refers to the *Collected Works*, with the corresponding number, name of the volume, publication date, and page number.

4. Judith Herman, op.cit., p.7–31.

5. See Camille Paglia, *Sex, Art, and American Culture* (New York: Random House, 1992), and Kate Roiphe, *The Morning After: Fear, Sex & Feminism on College Campuses* (New York: Little, Brown & Co., 1993).

6. Stanley Crouch, quoted in A.S. Ross, "Are We a Nation of Victims?" *San Francisco Examiner*, December 13, 1992, D 1-6.

7. See Wendy Kaminer, *I'm Dysfunctional, You're Dysfunctional: The Recovery Movement and other Self-Help Fashions* (Redding, MA: Addison-Wesley, 1993).

8. See Charles Sykes, *A Nation of Victims: The Decay of the American Character* (New York: St Martin's, 1993).

9. Ibid.

10. A. B. Ross, "Are We a Nation of Victims?" *San Francisco Examiner,* December 13, 1992, D 6.

11. Charles Sykes, quoted in A.S. Ross, "Are We a Nation of Victims?" *San Francisco Examiner*, December 13, 1992, D 1-6.

12. "The Unraveling of a Torrid Tale," *U.S. News and World Report*, 27 June 1988, p.10.

13. See Gloria Steinem, *Revolution from Within: A Book of Self-Esteem* (New York: Little, Brown & Co.,1992).

14. Deirdre English, "She's Her Weakness Now," *New York Times Book Review*, 2 February 1992, p.13.

15. Shelby Steele, *The Content of Our Character: A New Vision of Race in America* (New York: HarperCollins, 1991), p.57–75.

16. Richard Lacayo, "A Question of Responsibility," *Time*, 13 February 1989, p.68.

17. Annetta Miller, Patrick Rogers, Lynn Haessly, "Serial-Murder Aftershocks," *Newsweek*, 12 August 1991, p.28.

18. James Hillman, *Archetypal Psychology* (Dallas: Spring, 1985), p.1.

19. Don Johnson, *Body, Spirit and Democracy* (Berkeley, CA: North Atlantic, 1993), p.197.

20. C.G. Jung, *Dreams*, from the CW, Volumes 4, 8, 12, 16 (Princeton, N.J.: Princeton University Press, 1974), p.256.

21. Marie Louise von Franz, *Interpretation of Fairytales* (Dallas: Spring, 1970), p.1–26.

22. C.G. Jung uses and refines this terminology throughout his writings which span over fifty years. *CW* Volumes VIII and IX focus on his personality theory.

23. Sylvia Brinton Perera, *Descent to the Goddess* (Toronto: Inner City Books, 1981), p.96.

CHAPTER TWO

1. Karl Kerenyi, *Essays on a Science of Mythology* (Princeton, NJ: Princeton University Press, 1963), p.137.

2. See Joseph Campbell, *Hero with a Thousand Faces* (Princeton, NJ: Princeton University Press, 1990).

3. See Sylvia Perera, *Descent to the Goddess* (Toronto: Inner City Books, 1981).

4. Joseph Campbell, *Creative Mythology*, Volume IV, Masks of God, (London: Penguin, 1968), p.67.

5. See Graves, Robert, *White Goddess: An Historical Grammar of Poetic Myth* (New York: Noonday Press, 1983).

6. C.G. Jung, CW, IX,i (1968), *The Archetypes and the Collective Unconscious*, p.162.

7. H. Foley, *The Homeric Hymn to Demeter* (Princeton, NJ: Princeton University Press, 1994), p.139.

8. Jean Baker Miller, *Toward a New Psychology of Women,* Second Edition (Boston: Beacon Press, 1986), p.23.

9. Robert Hopcke, *A Guided Tour to the Collected Works of Jung* (Boston: Shambhala, 1992), p.107.

10. C.G.Jung, CW, IX, i (1968), *The Archetypes and the Collective Unconscious*, p.167.

11. See C.G.Jung, CW, VIII (1968) *The Structure and Dynamics of the Psyche*, for an extended discussion of the topic.

12. See Henryk Ibsen, *A Doll's House* (New York: Viking, 1965).

13. John Leo, "Pedophiles in the Schools," *U.S.News and World Report*, 11 October 1993, p.37.

14. Victor Turner, "The Liminal Period in the Rites of Passage," in *Betwixt and Between.* Mahdi et al., eds. (Lasalle, IL: Open Court, 1987), p.7.

15. Ibid., p.15.

16. Toni Wolff in A. Samuels, *Jung and the Post Jungians* (London: Routledge, 1985), p.217–18.

17. C. Schapira, *The Cassandra Complex* (Toronto: Inner City Books, 1988), p.147.

18. H. Foley, op.cit., p.134.

19. Marie Louise von Franz, op.cit., p.1–26.

CHAPTER THREE

1. Andrew Lang, *The Blue Fairy Book* (Magnolia, MA: Peter Smith, 1989), p.100–119.

2. D.W. Winnicott, "Creativity and its Origins," in *Playing and Reality* (New York: Penguin Books, 1967), p.97.

3. Jessica Benjamin, *The Bonds of Love* (New York: Pantheon, 1989), p.128.

4. See Alice Koller, *An Unknown Woman* (New York: Bantam, 1983).

5. Robert Hopcke, op.cit., p.126.

6. Alan Dershowitz, *The Abuse Excuse* (New York: Little, Brown & Co., 1994), p.3–42.

CHAPTER FOUR

1. The Reverend Jim Jones led his People's Temple congregation of San Francisco on a flight to mass suicide in Guyana in the fall of 1978.

2. Alice Miller, *The Drama of the Gifted Child* (New York: Basic Books, 1981), p.64–76.

3. Ibid., p.67.

4. Ibid., p.9.

5. See Cathy Rose in *Idealization and Disappointment,* unpublished dissertation, California Institute of Integral Studies, 1995.

6. Ibid., p.171.

7. Ibid., p.182.

8. Mary S. Whitehouse, "*The Tao of the Body,*" Paper presented to the Analytic Psychology Club of Los Angeles, 1958, p.23.

9. See Charlene Spretnak, *States of Grace* (San Francisco: Harper-Collins, 1991).

10. L.H. Stewart quoted in Joan Chodorow "*The Emotions (Psyche's Body),*" Paper presented at the North-South Conference of Jungian Analysts, 1990, p.11.

11. Tanya Wilkinson, "Returning to Mystery," in *Modern Renaissance,* ed. M. Compton (St. Paul: Llewelyn Press, in press).

12. See C.G. Jung, CW, XV (1966), *The Spirit in Man, Art, and Literature.*

13. Daniel Deslauriers, "Dimensions of Knowing," in *Revision* v.14, No 4, Spring 1992, p.192.

CHAPTER FIVE

1. See her books *Drama of the Gifted Child* (New York: Basic Books, 1981) and *Thou Shalt Not Be Aware: Society's Betrayal of the Child* (New York: Dutton, 1988).

2 Sylvia Brinton Perera, *The Scapegoat Complex* (Toronto: Inner City Books, 1986), p.50.

3. Ibid., p.51.

4. Ibid., p.52.

CHAPTER SIX

1. Judith Herman, *Trauma and Recovery* (New York: Basic Books, 1992), p.82.

2. Ron Messer, "A Jungian Interpretation of the Relationship of Culture, Hero and Trickster," in *Studies in Religion*, V.II, No.3, p.310.

3. Judith Herman, op.cit., p.75.

4. Ibid., p.79.

5. Ibid., p.77.

6. Ibid., p.77.

7. Ibid., p.93.

8. Ibid., p.81.

9. Ibid., p.80.

10. Ibid., p.94.

11. C.G. Jung, CW, IV (1985) *Freud and Psychoanalysis*, p.255.

12. See Judith Herman (op.cit., p.79) on the coping behavior of political prisoners.

13. C.G. Jung, CW, IX, i (1968), *The Archetypes and the Collective Unconscious*, p.271.

14. See Jessica Benjamin, *The Bonds of Love* (New York: Pantheon, 1988).

15. Judith Herman, op.cit., p.93.

16. Ibid., p.83.

17. Ron Messer, op.cit., p.319.

18. C.G. Jung quoted in Robert Bosnak, *A Little Course in Dreams* (Boston: Shambhala, 1993), p.64.

19. C.G. Jung, CW, XV (1966) *The Spirit in Man, Art, and Literature*, p.94.

CHAPTER SEVEN

1. V. Mansfeld, "The Opposites in Quantum Physics and Jungian Psychology," *Journal of Analytic Psychology*, 36(2), 1991, p.289–306.

2. C.G. Jung, CW, X (1970), *Civilization in Transition,* p.337.

3. See Jean Baker Miller, *Toward a New Psychology of Women*, Second Edition (Boston: Beacon Press, 1986) and Jessica Benjamin, *The Bonds of Love* (New York: Pantheon, 1988).

4. See the Big Book of AA, which is entitled *Alcoholics Anonymous* (New York: Alcoholics Anonymous World Service, 1976).

5. Edward Edinger, *Ego and Archetype* (New York: Penguin, 1986), p.5–7.

6. Mary Gaitskill, "On Not Being a Victim," *Harper's*, March 1994, p.42.

7. Ibid., p.39.

8. See Marie Louise von Franz, *Interpretation of Fairytales* (Dallas: Spring Publications, 1970), p.32.

9. Ibid., p.42.

10. C.G. Jung, CW, XV (1966), *The Spirit in Man, Art, and Literature*, p.95.

CHAPTER EIGHT

1. Joseph Campbell, *The Power of Myth* (New York: Doubleday, 1988), p.129.

2. The oldest known versions of the descent motif have three features that are important to this discussion: 1) the protagonist chooses to descend; 2) the descent is to a chthonic realm that is pictured and graspable, a place which has a connection to the Upperworld, even if traversing that connection involves considerable suffering; 3) the journeys are resolved through the establishment of an ongoing cycle of descent and return which is shared by male and female figures. The descent of Inanna, the Sumerian Queen of Heaven, is probably the most widely known version of this older form. Inanna's descent is a story of death and regeneration. Inanna decides to visit her "dark sister" in the Underworld (the reasons for this decision are unclear, probably because of the fragmentary nature of the surviving clay tablets on which the myth is written). The dark sister is Ereshkigal, a Goddess with clear qualities and strong emotions. The myth describes in detail how Inanna surrenders to an excruciating, dismembering initiation into the Underworld. The Underworld is not vague, nor is its ruling goddess. Ereshkigal gives birth while Inanna is suffering dismemberment, and a male god of the Upperworld mediates her relationship with Inanna through emissaries who empathize with the dark sister's birth pangs. Inanna returns to the Upperworld in a transfigured state with new attitudes and different powers. An ongoing cycle of descent and return is established in which a male descends for six months of the year and then is replaced by a female for the remaining half of the year.

The implications for worldview in this myth are several. Inanna chooses to make herself vulnerable to the chthonic powers of the Underworld, even though her initiation into Ereshkigal's realm is torturous. The Underworld becomes known to her; it is possible to tolerate disintegration there and then, reintegration to a transformed state. This happens through specific acts. Such a story can provide a sense that it is possible to make a relationship to the Underworld. The Underworld still holds death, pain and intense vulnerability, but it is a negotiable realm. It also is a place in which birth is possible, both the birth of Ereshkigal's baby and the rebirth of Inanna. The opposites are not so strictly separated; life and death are pictured as interwoven. Gender roles are varied here—Ereshkigal is very aggressive, while sympathetic mediation is initiated by a male figure. The cycle of descent and return is borne by both genders. The world view reflected in this story portrays experiences of suffering, injustice and loss, the human experiences which take one to the Underworld, as bearable, meaningful, and natural. The myth portrays responses to suffering, such as surrender and empathy, which will further the resolution of suffering. The emotional aspects of maintaining relationships are the province of both sexes, as is the symbolic job of being vulnerable to the cycles of nature, the eternal descent and return.

Beginning with Hades's tenure as the Lord of Hell, the forces of the Underworld, which may break destructively upon the Upperworld at any capricious moment, are commanded by a figure who cannot be known, who is invisible, who provides the mortal human being with no way of making a relationship to the Underworld. Hades rules a kingdom which, in earlier mythic cycles, belonged to the great Goddesses of Death and Regeneration like Ereshkigal. The primordial motif of the Destroyer/Regenatrix portrays, in female imagery, the linked cosmic forces of destruction and creation.[a] These earlier rulers of the realm of death, as we have seen in Inanna's story, have distinct characteristics and play an active role. Details concerning the Goddess's life and attributes abound in her own myth and in myths which involve the Underworld journeys of others. The cosmic Goddess of Death and Regeneration, who embodied the medial connection between destruction and rebirth, whose characteristics and realm portrayed the paradoxical way in which potential is inherent in disintegration, gave way to a featureless force of Death, to whom regeneration is only an encroachment on his property. Consequently the experiences of disintegration and death are separated from the experiences of regeneration and life.

> **a.** See Marija Gimbutas, *The Language of the Goddess* (San Francisco: HarperCollins, 1989).

3. L. Foley, *The Homeric Hymn to Demeter* (Princeton, NJ: Princeton University Press, 1994), p.111–118.

4. Ibid., p.111–118.

5. Robert Graves, *The Greek Myths,* Volume II (Middlesex: Penguin, 1975), p.393.

6. See James G. Fraser, *The Golden Bough: A Study in Magic and Religion* (New York: MacMillan, 1960).

7. Christine Downing, "Persephone in Hades," *Anima*, v.4, 1977, p.22–29.

8. Foley, op.cit., p.115.

9. Ibid., p.89.

10. This is a restitution of what had been a vivid aspect of the Goddess in pre-patriarchal mythology. Persephone becomes the Terrible Mother, the dark face of the Destroyer/Regenatrix and as such her image reaches back through time to Catal Huyuk. "The beginning of the concept of continuous life/death duality and of divine ambivalence, expressed in ancient Greek mythical images such as . . . Demeter-Kore or Persephone, goes back to the Neolithic-Chalcolithic era (7000 B.C.–3500 B.C.)."[a] Persephone becomes the Underworld reflection of Demeter, restoring the patriarchally-denied, Dark aspects of the Triple Goddess to a composite Divine Mother. The Neolithic "Goddess of regeneration, i.e., a Moon Goddess . . . encompassing the archetypal unity and multiplicity of feminine nature. . . . wielder of the destructive powers of nature,"[b] persists in Classical Greece as a bonded pair, consisting of Demeter and the transformed Kore who is Persephone.

a. Marija Gimbutas, *Goddesses and Gods of Old Europe* (Berkeley: University of California Press, 1974) p.163.

b. Ibid., p.152.

11. Wilhelm Otto, "The Meaning of the Eleusinian Mysteries," in J.L.Campbell, editor, *The Mysteries* (Princeton, NJ: Princeton University Press, 1955), p.30.

12. Marija Gimbutas, *The Language of the Goddess* (San Francisco: HarperCollins, 1989), p.208–211.

13. The Richard Bey show regularly has a "payback" feature which may consist of public confrontation or, in situations where the villain of the story is cooperative enough, an actual physical revenge. This involves strapping the acknowledged perpetrator to a revolving platform and allowing the victim to cover him or her with gooey substances such as peanut butter.

14. Elaine Pagels, *Adam, Eve, and the Serpent* (New York: Vintage, 1989), p.147.

15. The great creation narratives of the West, whether religious, philosophical or scientific, share a vision in which the most essential and important aspects of life are transcendent. Beginning with the Greeks we find that "the best things about the world are somehow not of the world."[a] Man's place in this worldview is that of the subject, seeking identification with orderly, transcendent, rational ideals. Woman's place has been that of the object, a shadowy "other" paradoxically embodying the horrors of chaos and the magic of lost connection. The epistemological split between subject and object, with its attendant illusion of objective or impersonal knowledge, is a gendered split as many have pointed out (i.e. Keller, Benjamin). The dominant worldview springing from and supported by this premise diminishes, demeans, and disempowers body, nature, and woman as interrelated aspects of chaotic matter.

This collective shadow is identified with the feminine, which becomes the receptacle of Otherness. In Jungian terms, women become the cultural shadow carriers, both in everyday life and in imaginal life. This is especially true of the shadow aspects of the victim's descent. The association of the feminine with immanent as opposed to transcendent values, with the body and with nature amplifies the association of the feminine with vulnerability, loss, and surrender.

a. Naomi Goldenberg, *Returning Words to Flesh* (Boston: Beacon Press, 1990), p. 206.

16. See Luce Irrigary, *Speculum of the Other Woman* (Ithaca, NY: Cornell University Press, 1985).

17. Charlene Spretnak, "Embodied, Embedded Philosophy," in *Open Eye*, 12,1, 1995, p.4–6.

18. See Wendy Kaminer, *It's All the Rage* (New York: Addison-Wesley, 1995).

19. Received secular wisdom in the West depicts a cosmos which can only be approached through the medium of rational understanding. "We overestimate material causation and believe that it alone affords us a true explanation of life."[a] Within this worldview the phenomenal universe is split into two aspects—that which we have explained and that which we are in the process of researching. As a pragmatically enlightened people we travel down the linear road of time acquiring knowledge of, and therefore mastery of, a fundamentally mechanistic cosmos. Human cognition is the essence of awareness. Insights which might question the primacy of linear understanding, such as chaos theory or the delineation of the unconscious, are regularly repositioned so that they appear to support the quest for a full rational explanation of the universe. All those aspects of the universe and the human being which are not particularly amenable to rational analysis, which are in fact mysterious, assume non-reality.

Mystery is merely a misperception springing from inadequate research. We "limit the definition of reality to the body of theoretical and empirical knowledge at our disposal and declare as meaningless all (other) questions."[b] Experiences and inquiries which resist the process of linear assessment, experiences which are perhaps nonrational in nature, assume a shadow existence within the culture and within the individual. The ego is the subject and the universe is the object. Habitual consciousness in the normally adapted Western individual is necessarily one sided, dominated by an ego concerned with relating effectively to external, consensual reality. Normative truth in the West is heavily masculinized, intellectualized, positivistic and materialistic. Consequently much of human experience that is mysterious, boundaryless, feminine, emotional, spiritual, and raw lives in the unconscious, usually in an undifferentiated state with a shadowy cast. In the western world the typical world picture and the typical individual are split between an acknowledged hyper-rational, heroic ego ideal and unacknowledged, unvalued, mysterious shadow. Jessica Benjamin, building on Weber's analysis, speaks of this alienation as disenchantment, which she defines as the "impersonality and neutrality bred by rationalization." Benjamin goes on to point out that disenchantment "inevitably stimulates the search for re-enchantment."[c] The persistence and ubiquity of the story of the victim's journey to the Underworld represents, I believe, an unconscious attempt to re-enchant life through a transformative descent.

- **a.** C.G. Jung, CW, XII (1968), *Psychology and Alchemy* Paragraph 657.
- **b.** Evelyn Fox Keller, *Reflections on Gender and Science* (New Haven, CT: Yale University Press, 1985), p.147.
- **c.** Jessica Benjamin, *The Bonds of Love* (New York: Pantheon, 1988), p.206.

20. C.G. Jung quoted in W. McGuire, ed., *C.G.Jung Speaking* (London: Pan Books, 1978), p.284.

21. Henry Gates, "Thirteen Ways of Looking at a Black Man," in *The New Yorker*, 23 October 1995, p.65.

22. David Ulansey quoted in Candace Chase, "Opening to the Numinous: An Interview with David Ulansey," in *Open Eye*, 12, 1, 1995, p.9–20.

23. Anthony Walton quoted in W. Morris, "Delta Blues," in the *New York Times Book Review*, 11 February 1996, p.10; Joseph Campbell, *The Power of Myth* (New York: Doubleday, 1988), p.129.

INDEX

S

ABOUT THE AUTHOR

Tanya Wilkinson is Professor of Psychology and Core Faculty Member at the California Institute of Integral Studies in San Francisco and a licensed psychotherapist in private practice. Specializing in women's issues and Jungian psychology, Dr. Wilkinson provides clinical training and supervision, conducts workshops, and has received the Distinguished Teaching Award at CIIS. In addition to teaching, writing, and counseling, she is an accomplished fine artist. Dr. Wilkinson received her Ph.D. in Psychology from the California School of Professional Psychology. She resides in San Francisco, California.

PageMill Press publishes books in the field of psychology and personal growth. Our publications are intended to intellectually challenge and spiritually enlighten the reader to self reflection, growing consciousness and the integration of body, soul and mind. The focus of our books is on the mind/body connection, the power of story and myth in illuminating the dynamics of our psyche and culture, the use of dreams in the movement toward wholeness, the role of the unconscious in human interactions, an increased awareness of the body in all of life's activities, and the universal desire for authentic spiritual experience.

For a catalog of our publications or editorial submissions, please write:

PageMill Press
2716 Ninth Street
Berkeley, CA 94710
Phone: (510) 848-3600
Fax: (510) 848-1326
E-mail: Circulus@aol.com